The AI Revolution

Daniel Vargas-Gomez

The AI Revolution

What Creativity Could Look Like in 2035

palgrave
macmillan

Daniel Vargas-Gomez
Erasmus University Rotterdam
Amsterdam, The Netherlands

ISBN 978-3-032-01171-8 ISBN 978-3-032-01172-5 (eBook)
https://doi.org/10.1007/978-3-032-01172-5

This Palgrave Macmillan imprint is published by the registered company Springer Nature Switzerland AG.
The registered company address is: Gewerbestrasse 11, 6330 Cham, Switzerland

To Justyna

Preface

Less than a decade ago most people's ideas about AI came from movies like *The Matrix* or *Her*.[1] Few could imagine that systems like ChatGPT, Claude or DeepSeek would become popular tools used by millions today and probably hundreds of millions in the coming decade. Despite the relative novelty of such systems, there has been no shortage of conversations about AI over the past fifty years. If we believe a uniquely human ability is being automated by means of computer technology, we commonly refer to it as AI (Manovich 2023). Still, AI remains a complex and difficult subject, and it's not hard to see why. When we consider the fact that "GPT-3 consists of 'a single system with more than 285,000 CPU cores, 10,000 GPUs, and 400 gigabits per second of network connectivity for each GPU server", such figures seem daunting and anything but self-explanatory (Langston 2020). Despite the overwhelming literature on topics like machine learning and neural networks, it's unsurprising that discussion about such topics quickly becomes overly technical, requiring readers to have knowledge of advanced mathematics, from statistics to matrices and

[1] The use of the term AI will stick to the definition used to describe the current state of AI systems available and should not be conflated with terms like 'singularity' or General Artificial Intelligence. In this book AI will refer to "a machine-based system that, for explicit or implicit objectives, infers, from the input it receives, how to generate outputs such as predictions, content, recommendations or decisions that can influence physical or virtual environments. Different AI systems vary in their levels of autonomy and adaptiveness after deployment" (OECD 2024).

multidimensional vectorial spaces, among others.[2,3] This, however, has in no way deterred media outlets, bloggers and influencers from filling our social media timelines with articles, podcasts and videos about AI. While devoid of complexity, they often provide little to no depth about a system's innerworkings, leaving us wondering whether they are little more than sheer speculation or advertising.

Despite its seeming novelty, the term artificial intelligence was coined by computer scientist John McCarthy in 1956, dividing the discipline along two approaches: symbolic AI and connectionist AI (Luitse and Denkena 2021, 3–4). Neural networks and their application belong to the connectionist approach, which attempted to understand the structure of biological neurons and replicate them artificially in the hopes of arriving at a stage where a machine could display intelligent behaviour. Connectionism is "theoretically rooted in cybernetic thought of the 1940s and was first implemented in 1957 when Frank Rosenblatt built a pioneering artificial neural network (the 'perceptron')" (Luitse and Denkena, p. 4). Its developments within the connectionist, neural network approach led OpenAI to release GPT-2 in early 2019, a Large Language Model (LLM) with 1.5

[2] From a heuristics point of view, machine learning is composed of an object to be observed (training data set), an instrument of observation (learning algorithm) and a final representation (statistical model). The combined use of these elements is utilized to describe how a machine can respond "accurately" to a human prompt. Using optical media as an analogy, Pasquinelli and Joler (2021) describes the information flow of machine learning as "a light beam that is projected by the training data, compressed by the algorithm and diffracted towards the world by the lens of the statistical model" (p. 1265). Machine learning is, therefore, a term that, as much as "AI", is used in a way that anthropomorphizes a piece of technology; machine learning has no direct relation to human learning as AI systems<Primary> work by simply mapping a statistical distribution, of a text for instance, from which a mathematical function is derived and expected to approximate what a human would comprehend from that same text. Notwithstanding, it can still be argued that "machine learning can, for this reason, cast new light on the ways in which humans comprehend" (Pasquinelli and Joler 2021, 1271).

[3] The term Artificial Neural Network (ANN) refers to the computational parallel of human neural networks. Strictly speaking, there is no parallel between human biology and ANNs. In its simplest form an ANN is a network of processing units which are connected to each other through a variety of nodes. This connectivity allows their computational processes and outputs to be the product of functional networks rather than the accumulation of independent processing units. This also allows them to store knowledge through those same connections, which is fundamentally different from the way in which files are stored, for instance, in a hard drive or from the way in which a software requires hardware to run an application (Guresen and Kayakutlu 2011).

billion parameters, followed by GPT-3 in June 2020, with 175 billion parameters (Luitse and Denkena, p. 8).[4] While impressive, the vast numbers of these earlier models pale in comparison with GPT-4, which is said to have about 1.8 trillion parameters, a number almost impossible to imagine (Raghunath 2024). Such eye-watering figures make the task of understanding neural networks unnerving, often convincing us that perhaps our human capabilities are no match against these systems. Figures alone, however big they may be, tell us little about what neural networks do. What we know about Generative-Pretrained-Transformers (GPTs) is that we can give them a set of inputs and outputs and they will find out possible relations between the two on their own, with no additional programming or guidance needed (Rational Animations, June 14, 2024).[5]

[4] AI Large Language Model (LLM) is a model that can process, analyse or generate natural language text trained on vast amounts of data, using techniques ranging from rule-based approaches to statistical models and deep learning. Chatbots, machine translation and the autocomplete in most people's phones that recognize speech are all applications of language models. Not all language models are generative in nature, and they can be large or small (OECD 2023). Language models are central to the way in which AI systems like ChatGPT, but not only, making an example to illustrate their utility relevant here. Language models work by estimating the probability of a word or sequence of words occurring within a longer sequence of words (paragraphs, etc.). Consider a sentence like:

When my alarm goes off in the morning, I ______ out of bed.

What a language model does is determine the probability of a word or sequence of words different words that can best fill in the blank. For example, a language model might determine the following probabilities:

crawl 9.4%
jump 15%
run 2%
tay 1%

It's easy to see, therefore, how estimating the probability of what comes next in a sequence can be useful for a variety of applications, from language translations to text generation as well as customer service chatbots, among others (Google 2024).

[5] Generative Pre-trained Transformers represent a different approach to Gen AI, particularly in the way in which they are able to process and use natural language. GPT models' main advantage is their ability to use large-scale data in a very efficient manner. GPT models can be, for example, pre-trained on extensive text corpora using a language modelling objective, enabling them to learn rich linguistic patterns and contextual information. After pre-training, these models can be fine-tuned on specific tasks, such as text generation, translation or summarization (Yenduri et al. 2023). In short, GPT models can deliver outputs that are much more likely to be accurate (if their training data is accurate), but also more convincing (more able to pass a Turing Test, for instance).

This means, simply put, that no AI system was ever shown how to play chess or Go, nor how to create images of cats or dogs. It has done all these things on its own. Inputs are run through layers of compute composed of channels, which are themselves composed of neurons.[6] As inputs go through these layers, each layer detects more and more abstract properties. Take, for example, an image of a cat as an input, which at the end is classified as a cat accordingly. Once an AI system has been trained on such data, it is able to generate new text, images, music or video based on a user's prompt or instruction. From a user's perspective, the experience of using current AI systems can elicit both awe and incredible frustration. These layers and channels appear to virtually any user as black boxes. Their function is not easily connected to the outputs we see, which has even led to the creation of unique brand of AI research called mechanistic interpretability.[7] To understand what each of these layers is doing, developers may look into each of its component channels and basically try to answer the question: what does this channel care about?

What makes it a black box is that even as developers can, and bear in mind the loose wording here, check what the channels are interested in, sometimes the response is not as obvious as it seems. A channel that may at first seem interested in detecting cats may only be interested in their ears or another one that detects squares may only be interested in right angles. The reason this happens is that the system is just learning whatever fits the data, it's not actually learning about pets, mammals or geometry. In other

[6] The term compute refers to the most efficient hardware and software architecture used in AI systems, which "includes one or more stacks of hardware and software that are used to support specialised AI workloads and applications" (OECD 2024). Higher compute means a system can work more efficiently through larger volumes of data.

[7] Mechanistic interpretability is a branch of AI focused on understanding the internal information processing of neural networks, akin to early neuroscience studies of the visual cortex. This approach involves analysing individual units and entire circuits within models to gain insights into their functioning. Despite the potential of mechanistic interpretability to enhance our understanding of neural networks, several challenges persist. One major challenge is the lack of a clear gold standard for assessing interpretability, which complicates the evaluation of different methods. The field also struggles with a lack of consensus on definitions and suitable measurement scales. While post hoc explanations aim to clarify specific model decisions for end-users, mechanistic interpretability seeks to understand the model's internal workings, which is a more complex task. Another challenge is that scaling models in terms of data set and model size have not led to increased interpretability. This suggests that simply making models larger does not inherently make them more understandable, highlighting the need for explicit models for interpretability (Welch Labs 2024).

words, despite the complexity of AI systems, their reasoning is limited, and we can never talk about an AI system having knowledge in the same way as we do of a human. To complicate matters further, unlike the one feature detection of the example above, what researchers and developers find is that each neuron can detect more than one feature about an image, a phenomenon called poly-semanticity. A channel that may appear to be activated by say cats and tigers may also be activated by planes, and researchers aren't always sure why this happens (Rational Animations, June 14, 2024). The challenges in grasping these types of issues have meant that despite much of the theoretical work about neural networks dating back decades into the past, the success we see today can be explained by scalability alone, scalability that was simply too costly in the past, given the hardware limitations of the time (Welch Labs 2024). Not surprisingly, progress of AI systems has not been linear, making predictions difficult and highly prone to speculation.

So, should any of this matter to a regular user? Should such technical aspects worry anyone outside the field? The reality is that while most of the conversation about AI within the specialized literature focuses on the technical and engineering challenges, much of what is discussed outside of it tends to be heavily idiosyncratic. Both utopianism and dystopianism underlie most ideas and expectations about AI. The fear of autonomous AI clashes with the utopianism of those who wholeheartedly believe in the indisputable benefits of technological progress. Industry and political leaders tend to belong to that second camp, making them strong supporters of Big Tech conglomerates and supportive of virtually any new technology, including AI. While talks about automation usually relate to manufacturing processes, generative AI systems that can generate texts, imagery, video and music are especially relevant to millions of workers in industries like film, media communications, marketing, design and music production.[8] Yet, serious discussions about their impact are obfuscated by loud voices promising that AI will unleash revolutionary gains, along with the democratization of creativity, where anyone can become an artist or creator at the click of a button. Qualifying and quantifying the impact of

[8] Generative AI refers to AI systems that can create new content, which may include text, image, audio and video, based on their training data, and usually in response to human prompts or guiding commands. Media coverage of generative AI has usually focused on the areas of text and image generation, focusing on popular tools like ChatGPT or DALL-E (Lorenz et al. 2023).

AI on human creativity is certainly not an easy task. A first challenge has to do with the multifaceted character of creativity, which seems at odds with the limited progress of multimodal AI.[9] Better creativity doesn't depend on productivity improvements alone. More productive workers are by no means more creative workers. Understanding the impact of AI systems on creativity demands that we fully grasp the value of creativity in today's cultural production and economy as a whole. It means understanding how such systems can be incorporated into a variety of different industries and disciplines, which is not as straightforward as many enthusiasts presuppose.

My hope for this book is, therefore, to present an in-depth understanding of AI that is accessible to a broader readership, interested in the impact of AI on creativity. The text will provide a detailed examination of the impact that AI is having and will have on the way we understand creativity in and through our cultural production, from the visual arts and filmmaking to marketing communications, graphic and game design, among many others. The analysis will be enriched through literature and research coming from an array of disciplines, including economics, culture and media studies, philosophy and sociology. It will also use insights coming from the specialized ICT literature, albeit translated into a language that is accessible to readers outside of it. This means that while not intended to be a technical document, the book will still provide some important definitions as well as dedicate some time to important aspects about the way in which neural networks work, especially, in relation to generative AI and terms like AI-art and AI-generated creativity.

Given the lack of a unifying definition of a term like creativity, the book will begin by discussing the challenges of defining creativity, through an exploration of a range of creative expressions from the past century in the visual arts, digital media and computational creativity. I will argue, in turn, in favour of rekindling common notions of creativity, to make the concept relevant to the multimodal expressions that allow it to exist today across a wide range of domains and be applied inside an equally large range of businesses. This means that from the outset I will avoid making a distinction between the terms creator and artist, which would force a split and a hierarchy along the lines of high-brow and low-brow culture. I believe

[9] Multimodal AI refers to an AI system that is trained and able to deliver outputs that combine multiple types of data, such as data from text, image or audio. This is done through machine learning models and algorithms and is central to AI applications in manufacturing and robotics (The Alan Turing Institute 2022).

such hierarchization is in the end fruitless, relying on canons of taste that, even if relevant in practice, remain arbitrary in nature. I will therefore use the term creator as an umbrella term that refers to all workers involved in creative practices, from a graphic designer to a poet. Lastly, despite its forward-looking title, this is not, however, a book about future supercomputers that will inevitably bypass human control. The book will argue that, while thought provoking, the subject of Artificial General Intelligence (AGI) remains far removed from the available technology, making it too speculative, adding little to a rigorous analysis on the impact that AI systems will have on specific industries, practices and groups of people.

Structure of the Text

The book is divided into three chapters, each approaching the topics of AI and creativity in an elliptical fashion. Each chapter will offer different perspectives, in order to study the different issues emerging from the incorporation of AI systems into creative practices across industries, including the arts.

Chapter 1, "Computers as Creative Tools", focuses on the question, can AI be creative?

It discusses the role that technology has played in shaping the way we define creativity today. It critically examines the ideological nature of the concept of creativity, stemming from a humanist perspective, which instead of clarifying the term renders it opaque and almost impossible to qualify. This first chapter will not only challenge outdated views on creativity, but propose, in turn, an expanded concept based on the ideas of Deleuze and Guattari and the theoretical underpinning of Bruno Latour's Actor Network Theory. It will show that not only is a networked approach to creativity theoretically sound, but is also consistent with today's cultural production, where creative outputs exist in a variety of formats and contexts.

Chapter 2, "Creativity as a Universal Aspiration", is a deep dive into the political and economic context around the new AI systems that have emerged in the past half a decade. It discusses the type of economic expectations that have been raised by the likes of Goldman Sachs and McKinsey, focusing on the purported role that generative AI is expected to have across a variety of industries. This section will also introduce the concept of the Creative Class, based on the ideas of American sociologist Richard Florida. Starting from Florida's ideas I will argue that creativity has vastly grown in economic importance over the past three decades and that it lives in our present across a vast range of industries, from game design to music production, copywriting and advertising, making it a universal magnet for talent and a prime target for the incorporation of AI systems like ChatGPT, Midjourney and Sora, among many others. Furthermore, Chap. 2 presents a critical overview of the economic context that led to the creation of today's AI, connecting both the macroeconomics of AI with the micro politics of the Creative Class, highlighting the potential risks and opportunities that workers in these creative industries will face in the coming decade. This section will end by introducing the idea of augmented creativity as a desirable and feasible pathway to incorporate AI into creative networks, while avoiding risks like job replacement.

Chapter 3, "Creativity in the Year 2035", presents a social futurology on AI, with a particular focus on the Creative Class and on the impact that the incorporation of AI across creative processes will have on our cultural production. Unlike common futurology on the subject, which focuses on the inevitable dawn of Artificial General Intelligence, such as Raymond Kurzweil's idea of the *Singularity*, my approach will be much more pragmatic. The focus of this section will be the examination of specific trends and developments, including job replacement and displacement, the massification of AI-generated digital content and the experimental uses of AI by artists, such as Refik Anadol and Jon McCormack. More than a list of predictions, this last part can be seen as an analysis of potential scenarios and as a critical reflection about the way we think about our own human capabilities. It will provide an invitation to rethink the way we envision the future of AI and its role in society.

Amsterdam, The Netherlands — Daniel Vargas-Gomez

References

Google. 2024. Introduction to Large Language Models. https://developers.google.com/machine-learning/resources/intro-llms. Accessed 25 Feb 2025.

Guresen, E., and G. Kayakutlu. (2011). Definition of artificial neural networks with comparison to other networks. *Procedia Computer Science* 3: 426–433.

Langston, J. 2020. Microsoft announces new supercomputer, lays out vision for future AI work. *The AI Blog*. https://blogs.microsoft.com/ai/openai-azure-supercomputer/. Accessed 18 Jan 2021.

Lorenz, P., K. Perset, and J. Berryhill. 2023. Initial policy considerations for generative artificial intelligence. In *OECD artificial intelligence papers*, No. 1. Paris: OECD Publishing. https://doi.org/10.1787/fae2d1e6-en.

Luitse, D., and W. Denkena. 2021. The great transformer: Examining the role of large language models in the political economy of AI. *Big Data & Society* 8 (2), 20539517211047734: 1–14.

Manovich, L. 2023. Seven arguments about AI images and generative media. Artificial aesthetics: A critical guide to AI, media and design.

OECD. 2023. *AI language models: Technological, socio-economic and policy considerations*. OECD Digital Economy Papers, No. 352. Paris: OECD Publishing. https://doi.org/10.1787/13d38f92-en. Accessed 25 Feb 2025.

OECD. 2024. *OECD digital economy outlook 2024 (volume 1): Embracing the technology frontier*. Paris: OECD Publishing. https://doi.org/10.1787/a1689dc5-en. Accessed 25 Feb 2025.

Pasquinelli, M., and V. Joler. 2021. The Nooscope manifested: AI as an instrument of knowledge extractivism. *AI & Society* 36 (4): 1263–1280. https://doi.org/10.1007/s00146-020-01097-6.

Raghunath, A. 2024. GPT-4 parameters explained. https://hix.ai/hub/chatgpt/gpt-4-parameters and Josh Howarth (06.08.2024). Number of Parameters in GPT-4 (Latest Data). Exploding Topics https://explodingtopics.com/blog/gpt-parameters.

Rational Animations. 2024. *What do neural networks really learn? Exploring the brain of an AI model*. [Video] YouTube https://youtu.be/jGCvY4gNnA8?si=rbcFLOnFVKO7O0zq.

The Alan Turing Institute. 2022. UK AI research infrastructure requirements review. https://www.turing.ac.uk/work-turing/uk-ai-research-infrastructure-requirements-review. Accessed 25 Feb 2025.

Welch Labs. 2024. The moment we stopped understanding AI [AlexNet]. YouTube. https://youtu.be/UZDiGooFs54?si=mGkBl3v9dx8of9Hz.

Yenduri, G., G. Srivastava, P.K.R. Maddikunta, R.H. Jhaveri, W. Wang, A.V. Vasilakos, and T.R. Gadekallu. 2023. Generative pre-trained transformer: A comprehensive review on enabling technologies, potential applications, emerging challenges, and future directions. arXiv preprint arXiv:2305.10435.

Competing Interests The author has no competing interests to declare that are relevant to the content of this manuscript.

Blurb

This book examines AI's transformative impact on creativity, blending insights from economics, media studies and technology to analyse its role in the arts and the broader creative industries. Rejecting narrow definitions, it frames creativity as an inclusive, collaborative process. Structured in three parts, the book first rethinks creativity through theories like Actor-Network-Theory, arguing AI is a form of agency within creative networks. It explores AI's economic drivers, citing industry forecasts and the rise of the "Creative Class", while advocating for "Augmented Creativity" as the right approach to balance human-AI collaboration. The book studies pragmatic scenarios for 2035, focusing on job shifts, AI-generated content and artistic experimentation—avoiding speculative AI hype. By grounding debates in real-world impacts, the book urges a critical, yet nuanced view of AI that ensures it remains a potential agent for collaboration rather than a replacement of human skill and imagination.

Contents

About the Author

Daniel Vargas Gómez works in the advertising industry as a Global Strategy Director and has a PhD in Philosophy from Erasmus University Rotterdam. His research interests focus on the impact of digital technologies and their role in shaping economics, culture and politics.

List of Figures

CHAPTER 1

Computers as Creative Tools

Digital Creativity and the Dawn of AI-Art

In October 2018 the AI-artwork *Portrait of Edmond Belamy* produced by the Obvious collective was sold at an auction by Christie's for US$432,500. The emergence of AI-art gains social recognition as auction houses like Christie's help it go from gimmick to valuable collectors' item. Examples like the Obvious collective raise important questions about the specific role that AI plays and will play in the production of artworks and creative work more broadly: what happens when AI systems can autonomously (or semi-autonomously) create work to be exhibited by museums and galleries? At a more fundamental level, would autonomous AI systems do away with the idea that creativity is the exclusive domain of humans and could a new type of creative collaboration between humans and AI emerge?

Creators and art collectives incorporating emerging technologies in their creative process is not a new thing.[1] Even when focusing exclusively on the incorporation of computers there are relevant examples dating back to at least the late 1960s. Computer-generated pictures can already be found in the work of Georg Nees, who used those images in *Gravel* (1968) (Rush 2005). Less than a decade later, Ed Emshwiller's *Thermogenesis*

[1] I will use the term artist and creator interchangeably, following researcher and artist Lev Manovich (2023, p. 2) who defined them as any skilled person who creates cultural objects in any media or their combinations.

D. Vargas-Gomez, *The AI Revolution*,
https://doi.org/10.1007/978-3-032-01172-5_1

(1972) mixed video synthesizers and computers to create imagery that appeared to dance against a sound environment made with a Moog synthesizer (Rush 2005, p. 95). More recently Hito Steyerl's *SocialSim* (2020) incorporated video game aesthetics and language, using them as key components of the work.

It would be absurd to reduce the work of Steyerl, Nees or Emshwiller to a simple category of creators who use technology. In fact, the work of these three creators is interesting, not because it uses this hardware or that software, but because it challenges the expected or prescribed use of the technologies it uses. Rather than an apologetic or naïve celebration of technology, their work challenges the mainstream or received view that conflates technological advances with human development.

Nees' use of computers, decades before they became so ubiquitous in our lives, was intended to open the door to a novel experience, a new way to look at the world through the "eyes" of computers. He saw in computers a unique way to visually convey balance between chaos and disorder, which was simply unimaginable for most people at a time where computers were mainly used to make complex calculations. A time when computer-generated imagery seemed rather pointless, given the hardware and software costs and limitations. Likewise, in Ed Emshwiller's *Thermogenesis* the use of computers appears as a way to criticize the intimacy and raw character of video and push the boundaries of our perception. It was intended to challenge the perception of "reality" that animated human drawings could deliver through this pioneering use of computers. Steyerl's use of video game aesthetics and language to criticize the machine-like character of today's highly choreographed social life and the need to be always-on and glued to our screens. The work also highlights how a life of ubiquitous social media immerses us into a world where our relationships are always mediated by Avatars of the other and of ourselves (Fig. 1.1).

Deleuze and Guattari (1988, 2008) used the terms deterritorialization and territorialization to capture the dynamic experience produced by contemporary art.[2] Deterritorialization refers to how an artwork challenges and critically deconstructs the expected meanings and relationships that determine what the technology can and should do, such as the, by now old, expectation that a computer is nothing more than a machine for solving complex calculations. One could argue, along these lines, that Steyerl's

[2] The terms appear first in Deleuze and Guattari (2008) *Anti-Oedipus: Capitalism and Schizophrenia*.

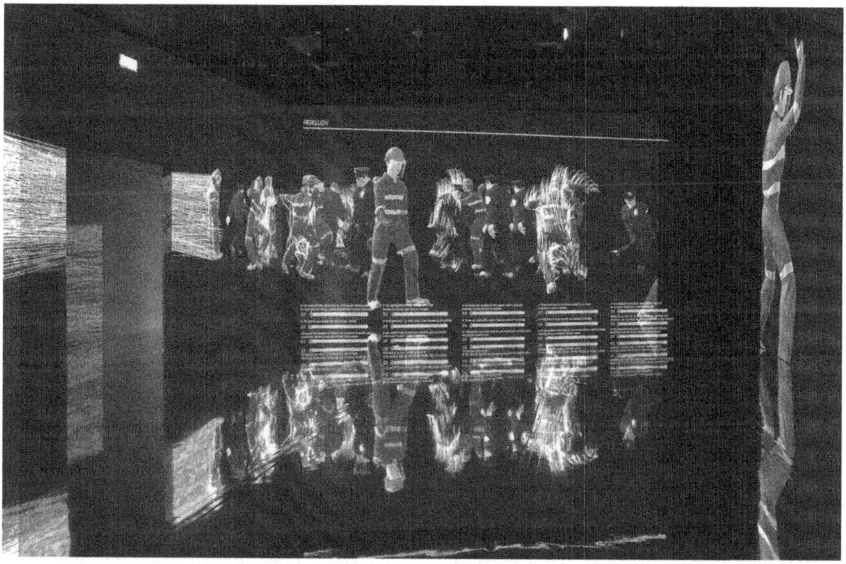

Fig. 1.1 Photograph of Hito Steyerl's video installation *SocialSim*, made for the 2021 exhibition *I will survive* at the Centre Pompidou. Photograph by Bertrand Prévost / © Centre Pompidou / Courtesy Andrew Kreps Gallery / Esther Schipper

SocialSim shocks the public, forcing them to reconsider the possibilities and potential new uses of video game worlds, avatars and the representational character of today's mediated world of digital imagery. Staying with *SocialSim*, this means critically assessing the impact that social media and video games have on the quality and quantity of our human relationships. Both social media and video games mediate our relationship with others, determining what it is that we believe about them and what we hope in turn they believe about us. The impact of such mediatization goes naturally beyond social platforms and video games; dating apps, instant messaging platforms, online communities, etc., are all examples of the same phenomenon. *SocialSim*, moreover, may invite us to be critical of the way we use technology to relate to others, but it goes further than that. It asks us to embrace the untapped potential that those same technologies have; they allow us to experiment with our own identity, they allow us to see the diminishing role of cultural and geographical differences in defining who we are and where we belong. *SocialSim* therefore invites us to rethink the role of avatars, while embracing the universal human experience that billions of humans around the globe today have with technology. In doing so, an element of innovation and novelty will always follow any initial challenge to our beliefs (Vargas Gomez 2015, pp. 38–44).

In a nutshell, deterritorialization refers to the event that allows us, as participants, to be freed from the social codes that dictate a technology's potential, so that we can rediscover its possibilities. This includes possibilities that may be seen as subversive, because they challenge the normative nature of our social structures. This means that social critique is but a first moment of this dynamic experience, which is ultimately intended to produce something new (e.g. new ideas, new relationships, new meanings). Once freed from the domesticated use of technologies, we as participants can envision new and tangible ways to relate to others and to those same technologies. This process of re-engagement is called territorialization or, more accurately, reterritorialization. Reterritorialization is all about creating new connections, new pathways to explore, new ways to think and solve problems, which, in many ways, pushes the boundaries of what is possible.

This introduction to the terminology of Deleuze and Guattari matters, because it's central to the type of event or experience that is missing in much of the current narratives about AI-based creativity and the uses of Generative AI (Gen AI) in particular. Fully addressing this point requires me to investigate ideas inside as well as outside the artworld and will be developed throughout parts one and two of this book. At this point, however, one should note that, unlike the examples mentioned, AI-Art like the one made by the Obvious collective seems to be entirely devoid of the elements of deterritorialization and territorialization. It doesn't challenge the way in which AI is intended to be used but rather conforms to the expected use of the system: where creativity is transformed into a problem-solving issue. The result being to put participants back in the role of passive spectators, whose proper reaction is to be in awe of what AI can do. The Obvious collective is, to be sure, not the only example of AI-generated creativity, yet it already allows me to point towards an issue that will come back, repeatedly, into the discussion: can AI systems become a true creative partner? Or can they even be creative in their own right?

Answering these questions without giving greater attention to the use of computers by artists or creators could narrow any answer to the above questions. Getting a better grasp of the creative ways in which technology has shaped and has been shaped by past creators will allow us to broaden our understanding about the role of technology in creative settings. My hope is that it will, in turn, provide the right perspective to envision a future where AI can effectively enhance our creativity.

Technology and Creativity: A Short Take on Computational Creativity

Computational creativity or, simply put, the incorporation of computers into creative practices began in the second half of the twentieth century.[3] It didn't begin in the workplace, which may seem a natural place for computers from today's perspective. Before Nees and Emshwiller, creators in the artworld had been experimenting with computers as far back as the early 1960s (Holbrook and Brown 1982). Researchers at Bell Labs pioneered the use of computers for creativity through a series of breakthrough experiments used to generate graphics, animations and art with early computer systems. Back then the research of AI was part of an emerging field of computational science called *Cybernetics*. The exhibition *Cybernetic Serendipity* at the Institute of Contemporary Arts in London explored a variety of novel and different connections between creativity and technology (Cybernetic Serendipity: the computer and the arts 1968). The exhibition included works of music, image generation, text generation and mechanical movement (Johnwilliamturneriii 2013). Creators like Gordon Pask, Bruce Lacey and Peter Zinovieff led the creative experimentation with algorithms and computers. Despite the limitations of the computer technology of the time, creators were still able to create surprising installations exploring, through different artistic mediums, three key aspects of our engagement with computers: the ability of computers to produce randomness, the ability of computers to transform mathematical or other inputs into images and sound, and the ability of a computers to react to physical stimuli, such as movement, sound or light. In all these experiments creators playfully explored the degree of autonomy, mimicry and novelty that computers were able to generate. Machines that would respond to different stimuli, for instance, through either sound or motion could convey a feeling of agency in the computer that was entirely unheard

[3] Finding a single definition for computational creativity is challenging, yet many have tried. A currently often-cited definition is: "create computations which—if they were made by humans—would be deemed creative" by the general public (Pieters and Winiger 2016).

of at the time. Such events not only defied expectations but also created a feeling of eeriness and unease in participants struggling to reconcile the idea of machines as pure mechanical tools with the idea of machines as agents of sorts. The exhibition pushed the boundaries of what those early calculating machines were supposed to be, and introduced participants into an altogether different experience, where the machine's output is not fully predicted but depends on collaborations, negotiations and randomness. Rather than the machine becoming a mere tool for a creator to use as they please, these works challenged the very notion of artistic intent, which is often perceived as the fundamental ingredient behind every piece of art.

In the 1970s one of the most active researchers in the field of computational creativity was American engineer, professor and advisor to the white house Michael Noll, who at the time stated that: "What we really need is a new breed of artist-computer scientist" (Noll 1970). Noll was not alone in his belief, which was echoed by creators inside and outside the visual arts, such as musician, songwriter and record producer Brian Eno. In 1975, Eno was one of the first to begin experimenting with algorithms to compose music. Eno would later describe his work as "using the technology that was invented to make replicas to make originals" (assistaOiR 2012). In other words, Eno was, following Deleuze and Guattari, deterritorializing the expected uses of algorithms and computers. More generally, Eno clearly saw the need for artists to embrace technology, but to do so critically, and with the aim of pushing the very possibilities that their inventors envisioned.

The popularity of these earlier experiments with computers was by no means restricted to the museum or gallery space. In fact, any history about the creative use of computers would be incomplete without mentioning video games. Video games became a fertile ground for the application of computational creativity in mass market settings. Around 1978, video games began making extensive use of algorithms to define game maps and in-game character behaviours.[4] Such use of programming methods allowed the industry to develop complex gameplay experiences in a relatively cost-effective manner. Extremely popular games like *SimCity*, first launched in 1989, took these ideas further, developing playful interactive simulations

[4] "Beneath Apple Manor", a rogue-like dungeon crawl released in 1978 for the Apple II, was one of the first games to have procedural generated maps and game objects. Available to play online at [archive.org]

of complex systems that could be run seamlessly in the home computers of the time. SimCity opened the door for the entire genre of strategy games, including its own SimCity series, the *Civilization* series, the *Age of Empire* series, among many other best sellers.

These developments explain why industry and academic research since the 1980s formalized computational creativity as a scientific discipline (Nicholson 1999). These experimental take on computer technologies sparked curiosity in less obvious fields as well: architects, designers, sculpture artists and computer hardware developers began experimenting with computational creativity too. It also has not been restricted to Europe or the US alone as exemplified by conceptual and mixed media work of Korean artist Nam June Paik, who successfully used computers in the 1960s and 1970s to generate music, poetry, movies, paintings and computer graphics (Pask 1968). The work of Nam June Paik has been very influential on Korean computational creativity. This is seen in, for example, the work of new-media artist Lee-Nam Lee, who reproduces the images contained in traditional paintings into modern Korean illustrations. He works by editing the images of classical Korean paintings, using digital software to insert, erase and combine them. In doing so he transforms classic Korean artworks into dynamic and energetic pieces that invite people to explore the meaning of the original motif itself. The purpose of this technique is not intended as a gimmick or as a way to simply grasp the public's attention. "Rather than parodying traditional works or implying a critical attitude toward the cultural reality of the time, Lee-Nam Lee creates a new story [...] his converted images expand the original artist's intentions [and] extend the narrative from the original linear image" (Park 2022, p. 78). The technology is used to reterritorialize the static nature of the painting as well as the historical context of the original, by allowing the contemporary viewer to reinterpret the painting. This is exemplified by his work New-Pak-Yeon Falls, which is based on an eighteenth-century painting by Korean master Seon Jung. The work is created using an LED TV installation that runs for 3 minutes and 50 seconds. Lee exaggerated and transformed the fall, which not only reveals the awe-inspiring nature of the fall, but he also attempted to express the sensation of the roaring sound of a waterfall that hits the rocks and leads to an echo using a sound setup. The power of sound transforms the Pak-Yeon Falls from a painting to an audio-visual experience (Park 2022, p. 79).

There Is No Place by Ki-Bong Rhee follows a similar approach, deterritorializing the idea that a realistic painting with a natural motif is meant to be a representation or faithful depiction. The installation covers the entire wall of the exhibition hall, where the spectator meets the silhouette of a giant weeping willow standing in a vague and constant fog. The artist visually captures the morning mist through a dreamy image that uses lights and water. The installation narrows the gap between pictorial representation and the three-dimensional experience by connecting them, providing an entirely new layer of meaning to the traditional ink painting (Park 2022, p. 82). While Lee-Nam Lee can be seen as revealing a hidden layer of meaning within the original painting, Ki-Bong Rhee uses technology to put an emphasis on what the experience of the original is unable to properly convey. “Ki-Bong Rhee is concerned with the fundamentally delicate balance between an eternal moment and a fleeting moment, while his poetic installation evokes a rare balance of sensuality and contemplative distance” (Kim 2014). In the work of both artists the viewer is invited to become an active participant and to co-create meaning through imagination—a dynamic shift from passive observation to active participation (Kim 2014; Oh 2004, p. 20).

A very different, but equally interesting example of computational creativity in the Global South is *Mestizo Robotics*, a collaborative, interdisciplinary project led by artist Paula Gaetano and architect Gustavo Crembil. The project explores the intersection of Latin American cultural and ethnic hybridity (“mestizaje”) and technology (Gaetano Adi and Crembil 2016). The project creates autonomous robotic spheres inspired by the Mayan creation myth *Popol Vuh*. These robots blend high-tech components (sensors, mechatronics) with low-tech materials (clay, organic matter), embodying a fusion of indigenous traditions and modern innovation (Crembil 2015). The work is meant as a critique of Western techno-colonialism in two main ways: by subverting the homogenizing narratives around technology as a colonizing means product of a uniquely advanced West and by celebrating the creative and practical aspects that result from blending Indigenous, colonial and global influences (Crembil and Adi 2017, p. 134). In short, *Mestizo Robotics* proposes a new vision of technology, from a tool for colonization or exploitation to a tool for cultural reclamation, rooted in Latin America’s history of resistance and adaptation. It advocates for a future where innovation emerges from pluralistic, place-based knowledge that celebrates the blending and mixing of the new and the old, the Global North and the Global South.

Lastly, computational creativity has also found a home in African digital art. *Stone Orgasms* by Angolan artist Keyezua is meant as a critique of gendered violence, using surreal digital compositions to confront patriarchal norms (Bisschoff 2017, p. 267). Keyezua uses technology to destabilize the normative character of gender norms, which are in themselves a product of Angola's colonial history. Challenges to tradition and the legacy of colonialisms also animate the work of Nigerian graphic artists like Williams Chechet and Udegbunam Tochukwu Bernard Johnbosco, who blend *ankara* fabrics and Afro-futurism, asserting hybrid identities that resist cultural homogenization (Bisschoff 2017, p. 265). Similar to *Mestizo Robotics*, these creators use technology to emphasize the dynamic nature of colonization, while challenging the stereotypes about indigenous people.[5]

The influence of the early work on cybernetics by people like Gordon Pask, Robert Breer, Roy Ascott and Jean Tinguely has been, to be sure, anything but a Western or Eurocentric phenomenon. Technology is used by creators from across the globe to contest the very notion of art and of creative practices. Their work continuously challenges the idea of the artwork as a fundamentally closed object, which the public could only observe passively and at a distance. Instead proposing an idea of art as "a complex dynamic system that provokes a dialogue between the artist and the public" (Apter 1969, p. 257). Stated differently, computational creativity shows that the work of art and the creative process behind it are fundamentally connected to the context from which they emerge. They connect creator and public to a historical moment, by enabling a dialogue that begins but doesn't end with an interpretation of personal artistic intentions. They propose instead a rethinking of the relationships that the creator and the public have with those same technologies and their potential role in our lives.

Their creative practices, furthermore, are as much the result of a web of connections as the work itself. Through experimentation, but also through research, the creator, which often includes entire teams of collaborators, is able to demystify new technologies so that instead of black boxes, they take the role of enhancers and transformers of human ideas and practices. Creators can in this way use any technology incorporated into their creative practices, not only to achieve an output but also to explore the web

[5] Likewise, works like *Awesome Tapes from Africa* employ diverse media—digital collages, interactive apps, video games and online archives—to enable polyvocal storytelling. This work digitizes cassettes to preserve musical heritage, in doing so merging past, present and a speculative exploration of Afro-futurism (Bisschoff 2017 p. 265).

of relationships that connects those same technologies to the public. In doing so, they point out how important the link between creator, artwork and public is. A link that is best captured through the concept of *network*.

The term network will be used here to refer to all existing connections between the creator, the work and the public. Through that network meaning flows, for example, as interpretations about the work's meaning take place. Within this network the public is not a passive receptacle, but can have, on the contrary, as much of an active role as the creator. We can see this both in terms of interpretation and in terms of reimagining how those new ideas and meanings found in the work propose in turn the potential creation of new relationships and new connections that lie beyond the specific link between the work and the creator.

The history of computational creativity helps us see how computers can be more than a set of new tools at our disposal. Likewise, it shows that contesting the image of computers as black boxes, whose inner workings seem technical and complex, is not the concern of systems engineers or software developers alone. By opening the black box, the creator helps the public discover new possibilities, which are not theoretical, but can be used in real-world practices (e.g. video games, design, image generation, etc.).

While unfortunately incomplete, given the many artists who have incorporated computer-related technology into their work, this brief digression into the history of computational creativity allowed me to introduce an important aspect to our understanding of creativity: the networked character of the relationship between creator, work and the public. A network that through these three distinct knots is able to connect meanings and ideas that can be extended beyond the museum, where the work of art resides, or the studio where it was made. Each network exists in relation to others. Their knots remain part of other networks, and their connection to others can vary in intensity and function; the public may become an interpreter and collaborator in the network that links them to the creator; they may be a mentor, a worker or a friend in other networks.

Next to its networked character, exploring the ways in which computational creativity took shape in the past shows the richness of the term creativity as well. While trying to present a stringent definition of creativity is not without difficulties, it remains true that the works discussed so far already show why the commonsense view that reduces creativity to a talent or skill is inadequate to explain the many embodiments of creativity today. The next section takes a step further: deep diving and deconstructing notions of creativity that are poorly suited to address the question of whether AI can be creative or what the impact of AI systems on today's creative spaces will be.

Demystifying the Relationship Between AI and Creativity

The book opened the conversation about the impact of AI systems on creativity by looking at how creators, especially those within the artworld, use computers as part of their creative practices. Doing so allowed me to explore the role that technology has played in their work, highlighting how it sways between being a tool and an agency of sorts. Yet, the images of sentient computers fed to us by pop culture make any mention of agency, in reference to AI, a topic that tends to raise a lot of eyebrows. Images of AI as an autonomous and capable agent that matches or even surpass human ability make the question of creativity feel personal and slightly threatening. They push us to consider whether an AI can by itself be creative, either now or in the future. AI creator Jason Allen, winner of the 2022 Colorado State Fair's annual art competition with the AI-generated *Théâtre D'opéra Spatial*, is unapologetic when saying: "Art is dead, dude. It's over. A.I. won. Humans lost" (Roose 2022) (Fig. 1.2).

Allen's words may feel startling, yet AIs replacing humans in all kinds of domains is an unsurprising admission nowadays. Thinking, however, about how a creative AI would be built often means reducing creativity to a unique skill, an innate talent or internal function that inhabits the creator. It's a common view, which finds its origins in a mythology that is as old as the myth of Prometheus itself, and perhaps even older. The work of the Obvious collective or of Jason Allen may prompt us to ask whether an AI with such "talent" can be built. Yet, given the recognition that these works have received, would it be a step too far to claim that the AI systems they used are already creative?

The view that all humans have an innate set of abilities, such as intelligence, creativity and emotions, which distinguish them from other beings, can be generally referred to as humanism: a term from which the humanities as a set of disciplines comes from. Humanism sees creativity as a fundamentally human trait and, in more romantic terms, as an expression of the human spirit. Under this light, artistic or creative intent and the expression of that intent become the defining aspects of what it means to be creative.

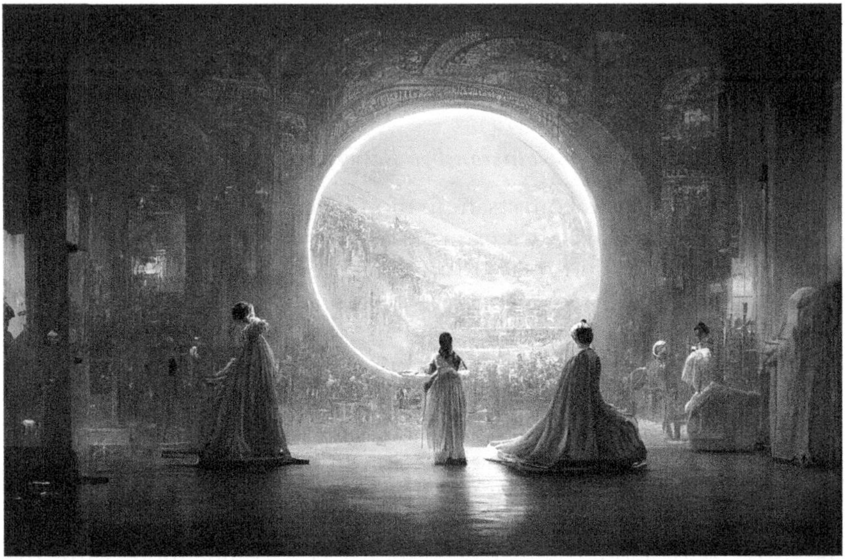

Fig. 1.2 *Théâtre D'opéra Spatial* by Jason Michael Allen using the AI image generator Midjourney to produce the image, on September 5, 2020. (Fair use of image without copyrights according to the USCO 2023). https://commons.wikimedia.org/w/index.php?curid=122602647

Following a humanist perspective, we can say that while Allen's *Théâtre D'opéra Spatial* is devoid of the type of social critique seen in Steyerl or the experimental character of the works exhibited in Cybernetics Serendipity, it's still not empty of human intent. Such intent is expressed in the form of so-called prompts. The term prompting refers to the way in which a creator provides the AI system, Midjourney in Allen's case, with a task to fulfil. The machine then translates the prompt into the generated image, and it's common for this to be an iterative rather than a one-shot process. Exactly what or how the neural networks translate a prompt into an image, in the case of Midjourney, or a text in the case of systems like ChatGPT, is not fully understood. While AI developers do understand how the neural networks operate, that is, how they attempt through pattern recognition to predict a plausible response to a prompt, the specificity of any particular response is not entirely understood. This means that, from a humanist perspective, understanding the connection between intent and the generated image is not as straightforward as asking a visual artist why they made a specific stroke on a canvas.

One could argue that what we are seeing with these AI systems is perhaps a deferral of creative intent. The work of American artist Jackson Pollock is exemplary of such type of deferral. Pollock's use of dripping techniques in his paintings adds a layer of randomness and unpredictability that can be seen as generating a similar split between the creator's intent and the actual work.[6] However, this is not meant as an argument in favour of a direct comparison between the level of intent in an AI-generated image and the intent that remains in one of Pollock's paintings is possible or much less measurable. Instead, one should simply take notice of how quickly an approach to creativity that is based on connecting the artwork to creative intent alone becomes problematic. Moreover, given that Midjourney, DALL-E and ChatGPT are the first AI systems to be used by the broader public, the more pressing question becomes this: what would be left of the humanist perspective's reliance on creative intent, when a future AI system generates art without the need for a prompt? Would we grant creative intent to that AI? After all, if it's true that AI has won, as Allen claims, then holding on to a definition of creativity based on skill would arguably confirm that AI systems can be creative, and that creativity is no longer the domain of humans alone (Fig. 1.3).

The scientists, developers and artists who have built and programmed past and current AI systems are not indifferent to the issue of creativity and have attempted to address the issue of intent and skill. This can be seen, for instance, in the heavily cited paper "Art, Creativity, and the Potential of Artificial Intelligence" (Mazzone and Elgammal 2019), a scientific paper that analyses the results of an AI GAN model.[7] The model in question is trained to reproduce art techniques from well-known artists,

[6] Jackson Pollock added an element of spontaneity, randomness and chaos by dripping paint over horizontally laid canvases, through different techniques whose results could not be fully predicted (Meyer 2022).

[7] Generative Adversarial Networks (GANs) are a class of machine learning frameworks designed by Ian Goodfellow and his colleagues in 2014. GANs work by creating a loop between two types of neural networks that simultaneously train and evaluate each other. This is an iterative process that improves the quality of results. More specifically GANs consist of two neural networks, the generator and the discriminator, which are trained simultaneously through a process of adversarial competition. The generator's role is to create new, synthetic data that mimics the distribution of the training data, while the discriminator's role is to evaluate the authenticity of the data, distinguishing between real data from the training set and fake data produced by the generator. The generator and discriminator are engaged in a continuous loop: as the generator improves its ability to produce realistic or convincing data, the discriminator becomes better at identifying fake data, and vice versa. This dynamic process enables the generator to produce increasingly realistic data over time (Goodfellow et al. 2014).

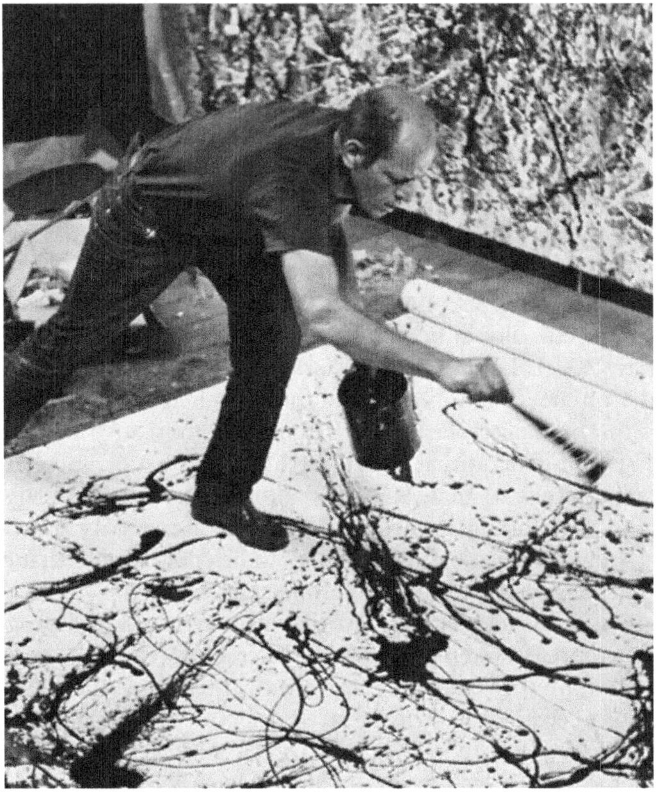

Fig. 1.3 Jackson Pollock painting in his studio in East Hampton, New York, 1950. Photography by Hans Namuth in Britannica.com. (Creative Commons / Fair use) https://www.britannica.com/biography/Jackson-Pollock

like Van Gogh or Picasso, based on a human prompt. Their initial valuation of the process and output delivered by the system is, perhaps surprisingly, that the AI in question is not yet a creator, because it misses the key ingredient to be one: intent (Mazzone and Elgammal).

In the same paper, the authors analyse a second and more advanced AI model with a higher degree of autonomy. In the second case, the system is able to generate an image without the need of a human prompt. Human intent is, strictly speaking, no longer needed for the system to generate a technically proficient image. The authors nonetheless refrain from concluding that this second AI is creative, by pointing to another shortcoming they referred to as the "lack of a natural reference" (Mazzone and Elgammal, p. 7). This second system, they conclude, is not yet an artist because it is unable to explore the world and use it as inspiration to generate art. The machine is not yet an artist because, unlike human artists, it has no sense data from the world "out there" that it can use to create an artwork. This shortcoming is less of a showstopper than it initially seems. Following their logic, it would be true that once an AI system is able to collect data beyond the one that it has been trained on, then it would no longer be limited by a lack of natural references and it would be, thus, creative. Although this conclusion shouldn't be seen as referring to a distant future, where AI has become embodied, but rather to our very real present where CCTV cameras, real-time microphones, satellite imagery, drone footage, etc., can all be used to feed data for an AI system to be trained on. In fact, one could make the case that all their current training data is external, which technically makes it a natural reference. It's all data generated by humans with access to natural references.

The question of intent seems to ultimately be a question about autonomy. In a way what these researchers seem to struggle with is the idea of a fully autonomous AI system. Principal Scientist at Adobe Research Aaron Hertzmann (2018) vehemently states that "AI algorithms are not autonomous creators and will not be in the foreseeable future. They are still just tools, ready for artists to explore and exploit" (p. 15). He emphasizes that describing AI systems as autonomous creators is irresponsible because it can mislead people into thinking that those systems have human-like attributes such as intelligence and emotions: again, placing the humanist perspective at the forefront of the discussion. Moreover, Hertzmann is not alone in his conclusion. Gangadharbatla (2022), Kirk et al. (2009) Lu (2005) all argue that AI-Art lacks the feelings and emotions that only humans can bring to the creative process.

Taking a step back, it may seem odd that researchers within this field would fail to properly problematize the extremely simple notion of creativity that informs their theoretical approach, but it's a step that they simply never take. Yet, there is an advantage in maintaining this humanist approach to creativity. Defining creativity as something that can neither be fully known nor properly described makes it opaque and essentially unknowable. If creativity is not really something that can be rationally analysed, then it cannot be part of the engineering puzzle behind the development of Gen AI models. This allows them to bypass the issues and keep their approach focused on the engineering problems: problems related to categorizing specific techniques and using machine learning to ensure that Gen AI can effectively reproduce them and verifying empirically that outputs resemble the style of artworks from distinct historical periods, be they the Italian renaissance, romanticism or impressionism. This allows their research to avoid some tough questions around intent, instead focusing on the process through which AI learns to learn a skill, mastering a technique. This is by no means an accidental choice. It's rather the consistent way in which AI has been developed and introduced in different social domains for the past 40 years. Back in 1997 IBM's *Deep Blue* made headlines, when it defeated chess master Garry Kasparov in what was then touted as an incredible accomplishment. In 2016 the machine AlphaGo defeated Go master Lee Sedol in an even more impressive feat, due to the increased complexity of Go when compared to chess. In both instances AI was not only able to match but also surpass humans at strategizing and predicting the probability of many future moves in advance. In a similar way AI systems that generate images learn how to master a technique: to proficiently generate outputs within an existing style, such as cubism or impressionism.

It's easy to see, however, that the question of whether an AI is creative is not at its core a question of whether an AI can imitate the style of Rembrandt or Van Gogh. Yet, reducing the question of creativity to mastering a technique informs much of the research around AI-Art. Mastering a technique may explain why certain humans can do things that others cannot. This is the way in which we distinguish, for instance, a virtuoso piano player from someone who has taken only a few lessons. The limitation of current AI systems is not their inability to reproduce a technique, but rather their inability to do so without a human prompt and even that may very well change in the future. This is why despite their best efforts to keep creativity safe from AI, the issue of intent keeps returning and why the idea of AI as an autonomous creator feels threatening. Likewise, and to our disadvantage, the creative practices, the processes and collaboration methods used by creators are entirely swept aside from their analysis.

Lastly, it can be tempting to look at AI-based works mentioned and think that what these images show is that AI systems can generate aesthetically pleasing or entertaining images, videos, songs or stories, but not art. These images, in other words, may be an engineering feat and fun to watch, but they are just not art. For them to be art, the argument goes, they would have to be deemed so by experts within Fine Arts institutions and places like the Louvre or the Tate Modern. This assessment would certainly make mastering a technique a secondary issue and AI-generated outputs little more than a gimmick. Yet, uncritically sticking to this conclusion amounts to little more than delegating all questions about AI creativity, to an elite, which would have the right and responsibility to grant or deny artistic merits to AI systems, just as they do with human-made art. It amounts to saying that the moment AI-generated outputs become part of a curriculum or are acquired by a reputable museum, then AI has become creative, and AI-Art real art.

Thinking about the impact of AI on creativity is evidently not merely a question of whether AI-generated images or texts or videos will one day be shown in the MOMA or the Centre Pompidou. It's not even a question of whether artists will be able to make and commercialize new work made in collaboration with AI systems; the auctioned piece from the Obvious collective already shows that both these things have happened already. What the AI models used in the examples above show, as well as the struggle of AI researchers to qualify what these machines are doing, is that the issue of creativity cannot be reduced to an issue about intent and skill.

A series of pertinent questions can help to illustrate why this is so: what happens to the value of creative work if, in the near future, an AI system is able to generate and deliver a stream of new cubist, expressionist, pop art or perhaps an entirely new style directly to art schools, museums, galleries and collectors? What happens when it is able to deliver a stream of websites, music scores or film scripts?

Such line of questioning shows that the role of creativity today is therefore much larger than simply a conversation among university deans, museum managers and famous artists. Its impact is equally much bigger than whether people will buy art pieces made by humans or machines, to hang in their living rooms. The impact of AI systems can only be properly understood from a much broader perspective on creativity. A perspective that in and of itself begins by challenging the humanist notions discussed here. After all, one would struggle to define the role of creativity in the work of Nees or Steyerl as based exclusively on intent, while completely ignoring their methods and tools—their network of creative practices.

This section showed why a humanist perspective, focused on intent and talent, makes creativity appear as fuzzy and ambiguous. It makes the work of Pollock, Nees or Steyerl appear less creative than the work of classic painters like Leonardo or Michelangelo, simply because the latter made their creative intent much more explicit. Rethinking creativity beyond humanism and free from metaphysical baggage will be a key task. It will, by the same token, allow us to escape the confines of the artworld and understand how creativity exists today across a variety of fields and industries.

Back to the Beginning: When Do We Know if AI Is Creative?

A humanist view of creativity that is based on intent alone individualizes the issue of creativity and ultimately leads to the conclusion that AI systems can be creative, in the sense that they are likely to match human creative outputs now or in the near future. Moreover, when the question of whether AI can be creative is framed within a humanist paradigm, it quickly becomes a question of judging whether a system or a human has been able to master an artistic technique. This perspective both equates creativity to existing artistic techniques and makes creative intent the core of the work, where it becomes an internal quality or talent. The previous chapter showed that analysing the role of creativity Steyerl, Allen or Pollock is not a neurological task, where comparing brain scans would determine who is more creative. On the contrary, any serious analysis of their work must be made with a historical context in mind and is judged based on their works' impact, not on any specific cognitive abilities. Creative practices are an equally important aspect, which is dismissed when we turn creativity into a uniquely human talent. Yet, given that in our daily conversations we often say that some people are more creative than others, maintaining that creativity is a universal characteristic of all humans seems to be, in any case, untenable. The humanist avenues to understand creativity obscure the question of AI's impact on creativity and risk relativizing creativity entirely, for it's simply impossible to look at two people's brains or DNA and conclude that one is more creative than the other without either of them actually making something. All judgements on creativity begin, hence, with a creative output that serves as a point of analysis and comparison. This section therefore begins by rethinking the question: how should we judge whether an AI system is creative? More importantly, does the question even make sense?

For this line of inquiry to help us further developing the notion of creativity, it makes sense to revisit the proposed networked character of the relationship between creator, work and the public, which was briefly touched upon when discussing computational creativity. To restate, the concept of a network was deemed appropriate to describe the relationship between creator, work and spectator, because it captures the meanings and ideas that flow through these three distinct knots, allowing ultimately for creators to challenge structures of meaning and power and for the public to see in such a challenge a repurposing of tools (e.g. computers) and concepts (e.g. a tool vs an agent). Like in any network, each knot remains connected to others, allowing for spillover effects: for example, a creative use of computers as part of an installation that generates sounds can lead to industry uses of the same method for sound generation in another context.

To better clarify the concept of network a short digression to develop the concept further is in place, following its use in the work of sociologist, philosopher and the father of Actor-Network-Theory (ANT), Bruno Latour.[8] A key advantage of Latour's use of the concept is the way in which it will help me rekindle the meaning of agent and agency. We usually think of an agent as a free and unconstrained will that is able to act upon a world of objects. Agent and object, it follows, are opposites; an object has no agency, no ability to plan and enact that plan upon the world. An object is just passive and can only react based on its internal properties: a stone reacts upon me hitting it by either flying away or by tripping me over, depending on its mass and the laws of physics, and the stone will never react by moving away or hitting me first. Within the context of art and creativity the creator would be the expected agent, but claiming that it is so exclusively raises questions about the agency of the public, given that the second can't be expected to passively consume, so to speak, an artwork. The work itself would be similarly an object and the carrier of the agent's message, which one would have to conclude is somehow embodied in it. There are more than a few issues with such a binary view of agency. Think, for instance, of the role that collaborators play in the creation of the work: a team of assistants, developers, editors and set designers, among others collaborating in the making of Steyerl's *SocialSim*.

[8] Latour choose the term network as a material metaphor that retains three important features: "a) a point-to-point connection is being established which is physically traceable and thus can be recorded empirically; b) such a connection leaves empty most of what is not connected, as any fisherman knows when throwing his net in the sea; c) this connection is not made for free, it requires effort as any fisherman knows when repairing it on the deck" (Latour 2005, p 132).

Would they also be agents? Or are they more akin to objects used by Steyerl to bring her vision to life?

More fundamentally, it's hard to argue that an agent is ever fully free of constraints or free to enact its will upon the world without limitations. It's also easy to see that an agent's ideas are naturally influenced by those of other agents, making it difficult to conclude with precision who would be the real agent and where intention begins.

Maintaining a strict separation between agent and object under such conditions is, thus, problematic. A more down-to-earth, more pragmatic, understanding of agency is needed for real-life nuances to be captured. It is precisely here that the explanatory power of Latour's ANT is advantageous. Instead of agents, Latour talks about actors. Unlike the all-mighty agents, actors are not expected to force their will upon the world without constraints, even at the ideal or theoretical level. On the contrary, their impact on the world is almost always done so through the mediation of others (Latour 1993, p. 113). In a network mediation is fundamental and the role of each knot is precisely to mediate between different actors. But if all actors mediate what would happen to objects under Latour?[9]

There is no distinction between objects and actors in Latour. There is a distinction between different types of actors, where every actor is a "medium of translation able to link the most far-flung objects and equally capable of failing short in this effort" (Harman 2009, p. 102). Latour moves away from speaking of agents and objects, choosing instead to talk about human and non-human actors. This allows him to qualify agency in a more realistic manner, capturing, by the same token, degrees of autonomy and the individual impact that each actor involved in a network can have.

Each network, to restate, is built through the relationships between a variety of actors. Networks can naturally vary in size and intensity, that is, actors within a network may play different roles and have distinct responsibilities. In the case of Steyerl's network of collaborators, she has a pivotal role in shaping the type of collaboration within it, but her collaborators are anything but mechanical cogs in this process. Their role as collaborators entails challenging and exchanging ideas, as well as providing

[9] "Modernity, argues Latour, has ended up creating quasi objects: 'Real as nature, narrated as Discourse, collective as Society, existential as Being: such are the quasi-objects that the moderns have caused to proliferate' (Latour 1993, p. 90). [...] Quasi objects are, in fact, neither object nor subject, but hybrids: half object-half subject" (Latour 1993, p. 117).

recommendations and changes to the creative process and expected output. The relationship between Steyerl and her collaborators is better understood if it's seen as a negotiation, where Steyerl's own creative intent is negotiated with that of her collaborators. The outcome of these negotiations, like with any negotiation, is not resolved by imposition, which means that the merit of any creative output cannot be reduced to the creative intent of a single actor and, in this case, be reduced to the ideas on Steyerl's mind alone. The beauty of the network is precisely that the ideas, concepts and meanings expressed in the work don't need to be reduced to the actions or the intentions of any singular actor. In a network, states Latour (1993), "nothing is, by itself, either reducible or irreducible to anything else. Never by itself, but always through the mediation of another" (p. 113).

Given the constant accommodations needed from the actors within a network, one can conclude that networks are to an extent fragile, in the sense that disagreements, disruptions and lack of collaboration will bring their inner flows to a halt. Conversely, the smoother the network, the more efficient it will be in its functioning and the greater the impact it will have on other networks; the better Steyerl and her collaborators are able to coordinate, communicate, plan, execute and, in other words, negotiate their joint actions, the more effective they will be at impacting the public. This implies that Steyerl is more effective as an actor, the better she can nurture collaboration within her team rather than impose her will upon them; their joint efforts enable them to identify the hidden potential of the technologies they work with more effectively.[10]

For ANT each actor can be safely defined as always having a mediating role. In fact, Latour defines three roles for actors: as intermediaries, as mediators and as black boxes. An intermediary is defined as an actor whose role is being a pure medium, merely communicating or transporting the meanings and energy from others, without modifying it (Latour 2005, p. 39). Simply put, knowing the inputs that reach an intermediary allows one to determine its outputs (Latour, p. 39). The word processor being used to write this book is an example of an intermediary in practice.

The second role of actors is that of mediators which, contrary to intermediaries, have a transformative role within a network. Mediators, Latour adds, transform, translate, distort or modify the meanings, energies or

[10] Stated differently, "[A]ctors become more real [...] by taking detours in their goals to capitalise on the force of nearby actants" (Harman 2009, p. 31).

elements that it receives from other actors. This means, therefore, that "their input is never a good predictor of their output; their specificity has to be taken into account every time" (Latour, p. 39). Many human actors in a firm, for instance, have a mediator role inasmuch as they are rarely expected to simply convey another's actor ideas passively. They are often, but not always, expected to add or modify them according to their specific role.

Thirdly, an actor can also behave like a black box. A black box means for Latour an actor whose interior is taken for granted (Harman 2009, p. 33). A black box opens the network to include those actors that must be taken by their full value, that is, whose transformative character remains somewhat unknown, but which cannot be challenged, changed or modified: "the internal properties of a black box do not count as long as we are concerned only with its input and output" (Harman, p. 33). For most people a search engine like Google is a black box, whose inner workings remain a mystery, but which they know will respond with certain regularity and predictability to their queries.

With this brief explanation of actors within the ANT framework, one can quickly see that creative intent is no longer the result of a single actor manifesting something into existence but is always the result of negotiations among networked actors. Furthermore, the question about the impact of AI on creativity is likewise a question about the role that AI plays within a network, where it remains to be determined if such role is that of an intermediary, a mediator or a black box.

To avoid excessive complexity, the text focuses first on the domain of the arts, before moving towards other domains, where creativity is arguably also an important characteristic of the work produced. The question of whether AI is creative can be rephrased as follows: what is the role of AI within the creator-work-public network? Will it fundamentally change creative practices? Will it fundamentally change the relationship it has with the creator(s) in such a network, or will it simply be another tool, functioning as a neutral intermediary?

In line with Deleuze and Guattari it follows that the encounter between public and work entails a two-step transformative process of a particular kind, referred to as deterritorialization and territorialization. This process outlines the encounter between the public and the work as a process of challenge and criticism of received views, followed by the opening of new possibilities, new ways of looking at familiar objects, like, for example, personal computers. Latour agrees with Deleuze and Guattari on the transformative character of such encounter, which he refers to as an event after which "all elements have been, at least, partially transformed" (Latour 1999, p. 126).

Such an event cannot be reduced to an aesthetics or to a pleasing experience. Seeing pleasure as the definitive characteristic of the event or encounter between work and public would amount to a form of hedonism, where the artwork is judged based on its ability to pleasure its public and nothing else. Such hedonism is encapsulated, for instance, in the cliché expression "beauty lies in the eye of the beholder". This expression fully relativizes the work-public encounter, confining it to a moment of personal consumption, which makes the idea of art being a social practice untenable. It also makes any conversation about art as meaningful as a conversation about good or bad hairstyles. It's a view that makes context and history irrelevant to the conversation, which it's been shown is incompatible with the history of computational creativity. Such a view is equally irreconcilable with the value or relevance of someone like Marcel Duchamp, whose work is heavily conceptual. His readymades, which challenge artistic norms and subvert the meaning and purpose of common objects, are seldom appreciated for their aesthetics, as they are after all common objects whose function has been subverted, but whose aesthetics remain for the most part the same. Norms, meanings and purpose are all socially constructed and become meaningless the moment the work-public encounter becomes another moment of consumption. Even in the case of visually strong creators the work-public encounter is always bigger than the discovery of an appealing aesthetic. Pop art creators like Warhol or Lichtenstein create visually stimulating work, whose merit cannot be reduced to their design or colour palette if we are to do them justice. Warhol's mix-media work takes the idea of repetition or reproduction and its strong associations with standardized factory lines and turns it on its head. Works like *Double Elvis* or *Marilyn Diptych* show how existing, many times reproduced tabloid photographs can, through the right technique, become iconic. Overall, Warhol's use and transformation of tabloid images into iconic artworks completely destabilized the idea of authorship and the idea of the creator as someone who makes something out of nothing. Again, the work-public encounter described has very little to do with a relativistic appreciation of the work and everything to do with the social character of artistic norms and its canon of beauty. For the creator-work-public network to remain capable of producing the type of experience described in the process of deterritorialization and territorialization, it cannot simply be inhabited by actors playing an intermediary role. A space for both participation and continuous flow of meanings and ideas between actors must exist for creative intention to be effective (Fig. 1.4).

Talking about flows of ideas, of social critique and of challenging established views may give the impression that the work-public encounter is mainly an intellectual exercise. Yet, similar to the reduction of the encounter to aesthetic pleasure one must refrain from reducing it to an intellectual exercise only. Take the paintings of surrealist artist René Magritte and his very famous *This Is Not a Pipe* artwork, which is often seen as having a

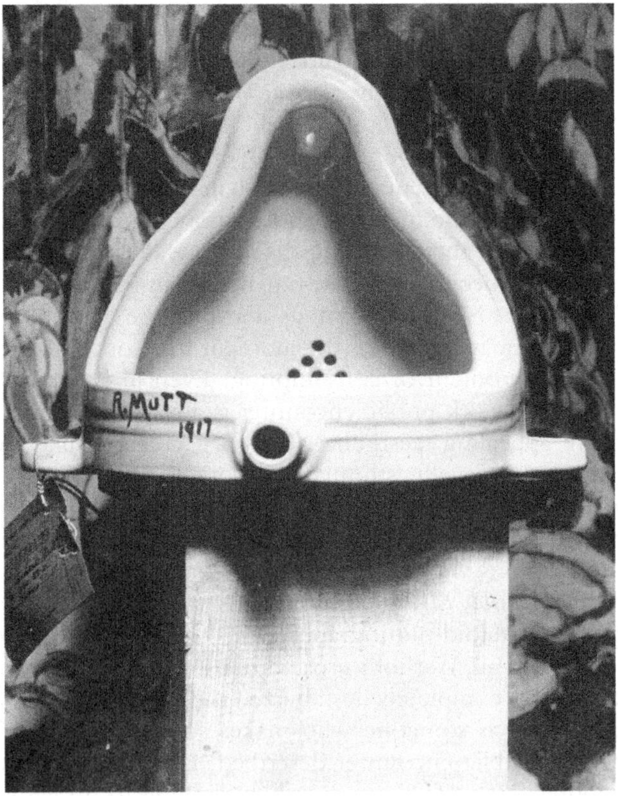

Fig. 1.4 *Fountain*, a 1917 readymade by Marcel Duchamp, photograph by Alfred Stieglitz. Wikimedia. Creative Commons / Material without copyright under Public domain laws

strong intellectual character.[11] Magritte's paintings are certainly interesting from an intellectual or philosophical point of view, because they resonate, among others, with authors who challenge the notion that language is little more than a representational tool, an inert medium used to transmit ideas from one person's mind to another. The paintings may indeed be evocative of such themes, yet they are not a visual translation of ideas that are extensively addressed in the writings of philosophers like Foucault, Wittgenstein or Derrida. To put it differently, what we see as creativity may very well have a relation to intellect, but it's neither a synonym nor a placeholder for it. It's an entirely separate concept, which, to repeat, is best seen as describing a unique process that may include strong conceptual overtones but is not reduced to them.

Along these lines, it's also common to see works of art as expressions of strong political ideas or political positions. Yet, once again, the encounter with a work of art shouldn't be reduced to an exercise in political awareness either. The work of Diego Rivera is not merely a visual representation of Trotskyism and Picasso's *Guernica* is not a journalistic depiction of a war crime. There is, to be sure, a link to a historical event in the *Guernica*, but we cannot equate the creativity found in the painting to its ability to represent the historical and political significance of an event.

While paintings and installations have been the examples used, the type of work-public encounter discussed so far can be equally extended to other creative outputs, such as film, music and literature. Marrati (2003) shows how Deleuze's work on cinema highlights exactly this extension to film when the latter argues that "in its greatest moments, [cinema] is capable of undoing that which our habits, needs and laziness have done, in order to make visible what the human eye is not made to see. But what cinema gives us to see are the perceptions, affects, and relations of thought that cinema itself was able to create" (p. 41).

It follows then that film has the ability, so to speak, to shake the ground under our feet. Yet its impact is, to restate, not confined to challenging our beliefs, prejudices or biases. It must again deterritorialize and (re)territorialize. In philosophical terms Deleuze refers to this as an expression of the modern inclination for the production of the new, the inclination to arrive

[11] Exemplary in this respect is Foucault, M. (1983): *This is not a pipe.*

at something different than what is already there.[12] Novelty is essential to our understanding of creativity and novelty can only exist as long as there remains an element of uncertainty.[13] The work of art, in this case, does not dictate to the individual what the right path forward is, but rather invites them to use the moment of deterritorialization to carve a pathway forward, which amounts to triggering a process of self-development, a way for the individual to go past the moment of critique into envisioning a new self, with a set of actualized beliefs and behaviours. The process remains uncertain because the individual can choose to dismiss the invitation, and different individuals may see the extent of their own journey of self-development differently. In Latour's network terminology, the actor's encounter with the creative output makes them aware of the networks they are a part of and of their ability to reconfigure their role or rebuild it entirely. Still, it will always remain up to the actor to precisely *act* upon such an invitation. In all instances discussed, it's essential to avoid reducing creativity to the ability to express a personal intention. Deleuze's ideas on cinema showed that we shouldn't reduce it to a particular medium either.

Just as well, creativity, whatever its form, is never truly grasped either, when it's seen as something that dictates a particular mindset or a determined set of actions. Activity or engagement on behalf of the public plays also an important role in understanding the work-public relationship. Activity is not the exclusive domain of the artist as the sole creator. As mentioned earlier the creator partakes in practices that are themselves relational or networked. Assistants, collaborators, co-creators, specialists, along with their tools and materials, all come together to bring a vision to life. The creative practices that organize these different actors are subject to change and reconfiguration as well. They are subject to trial and error, to discussion and to experimentation with different tools and materials. Activity, however, is also relevant to the public's relation to the artwork. It

[12] "The patent surplus of meaning and non-meaning that is present in contemporary art is a gesture that, rather than being merely the continuation of a postmodern critique of representation and modernity, celebrates instead, a modern inclination, which can be characterized as the desire for the production of the new, and for having something different from what is already there" (O'Sullivan 2010, p. 193).

[13] French philosopher Jacques Rancière states this point as well when saying that: "The images of art do not supply weapons for battles. They help sketch new configurations of what can be seen, what can be said and what can be thought and, consequently, a new landscape of the possible. But they do so on condition that their meaning or effect is not anticipated" (Rancière 2009, p. 103).

is through the artwork that the artistic network invites them to interpret, imagine and even play with the work at hand, sometimes metaphorically, but often also literally as in the case of Steyerl's interactive spaces or Yayoi Kusama's physical spaces.

The encounter that the public has with virtually any creative output is, ultimately, an experience or event that unfolds as a journey of self-discovery, where the sensual and intellectual stimulation cannot be easily split apart. The public is always confronted with a set of possibilities that either confirms and reinstates the world as it is or opens them up to new possibilities, new relationships and new networks. This is not a mental or theoretical moment, but the actual discovery of new types of configurations between humans and non-humans. Now, while the intention is not to make this text into a full-blown treatise on the philosophy of art, it remains fair to ask at this point: how is the individual notion of self-development compatible with the idea of changing or reconfiguring existing networks? How is such a process triggered or started? After all, it is individuals, not networks, who go to museums.

There is an important mechanism that is at work here: *shock* (Lazzarato 2010). Shock is the way in which we, the public, are awakened from complacency, the way in which creative work, like a work of art, pushes us to rethink who we are and what we believe in (Lazzarato, p. 105). Shock is, therefore, an effective mechanism of deterritorialization, because it allows for critical consciousness to emerge, and that consciousness or awareness is precisely what enables us to rethink who we are (Lazzarato, p. 105).[14] Shock is an individual experience; others cannot be shocked for me. However, given that actors are always part of a network (or many) what this means is that when an actor is shocked, their role within its networks is destabilized. Destabilization may mean changing from an intermediary to a mediator, for example, which effectively changes the relationship that an actor has with others; with other humans as well as with other non-humans (tools, technologies, concepts, etc.). In a way it's fair to conclude from Lazzarato's depiction of *shock* that understanding the type of creativity we see in Steyerl, Warhol or Nees is not about understanding what the created object is, but how it works: how it produces shock.

[14] In a more philosophical vein, Lazzarato (2010) argues that shock "[i]nvents a method for disentangling oneself from established values, including aesthetic values.[...] the production of subjectivity at their aim, the production of an ethos and a modus vivendi" (p. 105).

At this point the reader may be tempted to see my analysis of the work-public encounter as an attempt to uncover art's true nature or essence. This is, however, not the intended point. What allows the argument to extend this networked description of the work-public encounter to film, music, literature and potentially other domains is not the claim that ANT captures art's essence in a way that previous theories have not. The intention instead is to simply acknowledge that creative networks (humans, tools, materials) do not exist in a place that would somehow lie outside the publics' daily world of motivations, worries, beliefs, hopes and realities that determine who they are. Focusing on the work-public encounter, while momentarily leaving the artist role aside, was meant to clarify the ways in which the public relates to creative outputs. It helped to show that it's much more than a pleasurable moment, although pleasure is by no means excluded from it. It should also be obvious by now that it's also not an experience akin to a religious or mystical moment, connecting us to a transcendent realm. The work-public encounter is in a way a very down-to-earth thing. Its critique and its novelty matter because they impact the public's life here on earth, where networks endure or wither and where an actor's role changes in tangible ways.[15]

It's at this point that it makes sense to bring back AI into the conversation and the question of whether an AI system can be creative. It has been shown so far that understanding how a creative object works is more important than trying to define what it is. AI, as another actor within a network, will define its role based on how it changes, modifies or transforms the creative practices within the network it's present in and, more broadly, the work-public encounter.

The text highlighted the fact that all creators, no matter whether they work alone or as part of a collective, are always part of a creative network, networks inhabited by humans, but also smartphones, laptops, apps, video games, cameras, etc. If creators are part of networks, then this also means by implication that the markers of creativity so far discussed (e.g. novelty, experimentation, reappropriation of technologies) are fundamental to the relationships that exist within those same networks and to the outputs

[15] Curator and critic Nicolas Bourriaud argues as much when saying that "[t]he role of the artworks is no longer to form imaginary and utopian realities, but to actually be ways of living and models of action within the existing real, whatever the scale chosen by the artist. [Relational Aesthetics refers to] an art taking as its theoretical horizon the realm of human interactions and its social context, rather than the assertion of an independent and private symbolic space" (Bourriaud 2002, pp. 13, 14).

they generate. These creative networks are not identical, but what makes them different is not the use of a specific technology, but the way in which the non-humans involved, including AI, impact, change and modify the collaboration among humans and the experience of the public. Given that all creative networks include pre-existing relationships among actors, the introduction of AI will be judged based on how it challenges and reconfigures them.[16] This conclusion is relevant to any narrative about the role that AI systems will have today and in the future, whether they will replace, enhance or altogether change the nature of what it means to be creative.[17]

References

Apter, M. 1969. Cybernetics and art. *Leonardo* 2:257–265.

assistaOiR. 2012. Brian Eno, lecture in Rio de Janeiro, October 20th, 2012 [video], October 20. YouTube. https://www.youtube.com/watch?v=NePUAtTn8ks.

Bisschoff, L. 2017. The future is digital: An introduction to African digital arts. *Critical African Studies* 9 (3): 261–267.

Bourriaud, N. 2002. *Relational aesthetics.* Translated by S. Pleasance and F. Woods. Les Presses du Réel.

Crembil, G. 2015. Mestizo robotics. https://www.arch.rpi.edu/2015/04/f15-mestizorobotics-artx/. Accessed 30 May 2025).

Crembil, G., and P. G. Adi. 2017. Mestizo robotics. *Leonardo* 50 (2): 132–137.

Cybernetic Serendipity: The computer and the arts. 1968. Cybernetic Serendipity (1968, Aug. 2 to Oct. 20). Exhibition catalogue. In *Studio international special issue*, ed. Jasia Reichardt. London, UK: Institute of Contemporary Arts (ICA). http://cyberneticserendipity.net. Accessed 25 Feb 2025.

Deleuze, G., and F. Guattari. 1988. *A thousand plateaus: Capitalism and schizophrenia.* Translated by B. Massumi. The Athlone Press Ltd.

Deleuze, G., and F. Guattari. 2008. *Anti-Oedipus: Capitalism and schizophrenia.* Translated by R. Hurley, M. Seem and H.P. Lane. University of Minnesota Press.

Foucault, M. 1983. *This is not a pipe (No. 24).* Univ. of California Press.

Gaetano Adi, P., and G. Crembil. 2016. Guest editorial statement: Mestizo technology. Art, design, and technoscience in Latin America. *Media-N: Journal of the*

[16] This is why, in philosophical terms, Deleuze concludes that "contemporary art can indeed be critical 'but it can also plug into the creativity and fundamental productivity in and of the world that is ontologically prior to this capture" (O'Sullivan 2010, p. 194).

[17] Bourriaud's concept of Relational Aesthetics can just as well be mentioned here. He captures this conclusion when arguing that "Relational Aesthetics refers to 'art [that] creates an awareness about production methods and human relationships produced by the technologies of its day, [...] enabling to see them right down to the consequences they have on day-to-day life" (Bourriaud 2002, p. 67).

New Media Caucus. https://median.newmediacaucus.org/mestizo-technology-art-design-and-technoscience-in-latin-america/guest-editorial-statement-mestizo-technology-art-design-and-technoscience-in-latin-america/.

Gangadharbatla, H. 2022. The role of AI attribution knowledge in the evaluation of artwork. *Empirical Studies of the Arts* 40 (2): 125–142.

Goodfellow, I., J. Pouget-Abadie, M. Mirza, B. Xu, D. Warde-Farley, S. Ozair, et al. 2014. Generative adversarial nets. In *Advances in neural information processing systems*, 27.

Harman, G. 2009. *Prince of networks: Bruno Latour and metaphysics*. re.press.

Hertzmann, A. 2018. Can computers create art? *Arts* 7 (2): 18. https://doi.org/10.3390/arts7020018.

Holbrook, B. D., and W. S. Brown. 1982. Computing science technical report no. 99. In *A history of computing research at Bell laboratories (1937–1975)*. Bell Telephone Laboratories Inc. https://doi.org/10.3390/arts8010026.

Johnwilliamturneriii. 2013. Cybernetic serendipity (ICA) – Late night lineup (1968) [video], August 10. YouTube. https://www.youtube.com/watch?v=n8TJx8n9UsA.

Kim, T. 2014. *Imminent terrain*. http://immanentterrain.wordpress.com/2011/05/17/kibong-rhee-I. Accessed 20 May 2025.

Kirk, U., M. Skov, O. Hulme, M. S. Christensen, and S. Zeki. 2009. Modulation of aesthetic value by semantic context: An fMRI study. *NeuroImage* 44 (3): 1125–1132.

Latour, B. 1993. *We have never been modern*. Harvard University Press.

Latour, B. 1999. *Pandora's hope*. Harvard University Press.

Latour, B. 2005. *Reassembling the social: An introduction to actor-network-theory*. Oxford University Press Inc.

Lazzarato, M. 2010. The practice and anti-dialectical thought of 'Anartist'. In *Deleuze and contemporary art*, ed. Stephen Zepke and Simon O'Sullivan. Edinburgh University.

Lu, L. F. L. 2005. Pre-service art teacher negative attitudes and perceptions of computer-generated art imagery: Recommendations for pre-service art education programs. *Visual Arts Research* 31 (1): 89–102.

Manovich, L. 2023. Seven arguments about AI images and generative media. Artificial aesthetics: A critical guide to AI, media and design. *Artificial Aesthetics Chapter 5*. https://manovich.net/index.php/projects/artificial-aesthetics. Accessed 25 Feb 2025.

Marrati, P. 2003. *Gilles Deleuze: Cinema and Philosophy*. Translated by Alisa Hartz. Baltimore. John Hopkins University Press.

Mazzone, M., and A. Elgammal. 2019. Art, creativity, and the potential of artificial intelligence. *Arts* 8 (1): 26.

Meyer, I. 2022). Jackson Pollock – A look at the famous master of the drip painting. *Art in Context*, March 17. https://artincontext.org/jackson-pollock/. Accessed 25 Feb 2025.

Nicholson, Boden M. 1999. Computational models of creativity. In *Handbook of creativity*, 351–373.

Noll, A. M. 1970. Art Ex Machina. *IEEE Student Journal* 8 (4): 10–14.

O'Sullivan, S. 2010. From aesthetics to the abstract machine: Deleuze, Guattari and contemporary art practice. In *Deleuze and contemporary art*, ed. Stephen Zepke and Simon O'Sullivan. Edinburgh University Press.

Oh, S. K. 2004. A 'Study of Margins' as an acceptee's interpretative space-based on the expression of 'Margins' in contemporary Korean style painting. *Journal of Basic Design & Art* 5 (4): 13–24. http://www.riss.kr/link?id=A104164214.

Park, Y. 2022. A study of Korean aesthetic consciousness in new-media art. *ESPES* 11 (1): 76–86.

Pask, G. 1968. The colloquy of mobiles. In *Cybernetic serendipity*. ICA.

Pieters, R., and S. Winiger. 2016. Creative AI: On the democratisation & escalation of creativity, March 7. https://medium.com/@creativeai/creativeai-9d4b2346faf3#b28b. Accessed 25 Feb 2025.

Rancière, J. 2009. *The emancipated spectator*. Translated by G. Elliot. Verso Books.

Roose, K. 2022. An A.I.-generated picture won an art prize. Artists aren't happy. *The New York Times*, September 2. https://www.nytimes.com/ 2022/09/02/technology/ai-artificial-intelligence-artists.html.

Rush, M. 2005. *New media in art*. Thames & Hudson.

Vargas Gomez, D. 2015. Breathing Art into life. Doctoral dissertation, Erasmus University Rotterdam.

CHAPTER 2

Creativity as a Universal Aspiration

Rethinking Creativity: A Systems Approach to Imagination and Novelty

A simple search on job vacancies containing the term "creative" on LinkedIn returns over 1700 results, for vacancies posted in a single month, and only in the European Union.[1] These vacancies, in addition, are in no way confined to the art industry. Banks, Tech startups, marketing firms, hotels and consultancies are among the companies that claim to be searching for employees who are creative. This simple search, while hardly scientific, sheds still some light on the fact that today, creativity has found a place across a variety of domains outside of the fine arts. This is a relatively new phenomenon in the job market, signalling an important cultural shift. The term *creative* is quite a novelty in historical terms. Only until the eighteenth century did the term creativity become more frequently used, first emerging as closely related to a person's ability to display imagination (Tatarkiewicz 1980). In the late nineteenth century, theorists such as Walls, Wertheimer, Helmholtz and Poincaré began reflecting and consequently publishing their creative processes, in what can be seen as the dawn of the scientific study of creativity (Pieters and Winiger 2016).

[1] Such search results are algorithmically curated and time based, which means that it's likely that a search done by a different person at a different time may deliver more or less results.

D. Vargas-Gomez, *The AI Revolution*,
https://doi.org/10.1007/978-3-032-01172-5_2

AI and creativity researchers Still and D'Inverno (2016) examine the evolution of the term and highlight novelty as one of the key aspects defining creativity since its early days (p. 149). However, they continue, creativity was not seen then as a human talent, but as a natural process that would result in the emergence of the new in nature. This "new", in any case, doesn't refer here to the idea of making something out of nothing. Instead, it was meant to denote the ability to create something new out of the old, the new as the result of a combination and reconfiguration of the old (Still and D'Inverno, p. 149). This reconfiguration of the old brought along with it a certain unpredictability to creative work, based on the logic that for a recombination of elements to generate novelty, it cannot be fully predicted in advance (Still and D'Inverno, p. 150).

It was argued earlier that the role of humanism and its focus on intentionality biased the way we understand creativity. Remaining on Still and D'Inverno (2016) they see this emphasis on intentionality emerging in the nineteenth century, driven by the modern notion of the artist, which is informed by what they called G-creativity, that is, a romantic notion of creativity that presented the artist as a genius. The introduction of intentionality opens the door to the reduction of creativity to a human talent or capability, given that genius is intended as a defining term that captures the creator as someone who is not only able to act intentionally, but also autonomously. The artist's autonomy is essential because it's what allows them to overcome the influence of previous views, old ideas and, overall, break with tradition. Creativity, seen as a break with tradition, roots G-creativity in the enlightenment and its idea of progress as a fundamental and necessary break with the past.[2] It also solidifies the idea of creativity as an innate or acquired talent that rests on the individual. Turning creativity, in consequence, into a talent that only a selected few possess. It is during the first half of the nineteenth century that the, still common, idea of the creator as a genius takes hold. The genius artist, states German philosopher Arthur Schopenhauer at the onset of the same century, is someone who has not only the talent "to hit the target that no one else is able to hit, but [also] the ability to see the target that no one else is able to see" (Schopenhauer 1909, p. 158).

[2] For Kant "Genius is ultimately a manifestation of the vivifying spirit for, as opposed to the pedant's rigid adherence to rules, genius exhibits a free sweep of invention and thus originality that creates new models" (Gadamer 2004, p. 46).

The focus on the individual's innate abilities, with little to no attention to context and environment, is consistent with Cartesian and Kantian ideas, which see external influence as detrimental to our understanding of the world. In a similar way, emphasizing the outsider's nature of the genius, whose imagination cannot be grasped by those unable to overcome external influences, explains how creativity can end up becoming more ethereal, more mystical and ultimately unknowable.[3]

But can we really equate creativity to the talent of individual geniuses? The argument developed here has shown that such an approach to creativity cannot be applied to computational creativity or to many other artists, from Duchamp to Warhol. Next to this, such an approach to creativity forgets about the role of creative practices, dismissing them as little more than mastery of a technique. In reality, whether a beautiful film, a touching song or a fun, engaging video game, embodied creativity is rarely the result of a single individual. Whether in film, music or digital art, teams and collaboration are more often the rule rather than the exception. Creative intentionality cannot easily, if at all, be ascribed to a single specific actor. Still, creative intentionality and the idea of the creative genius, while theoretically weak, do highlight an important aspect in the modern view of creativity: the importance of novelty, meaning the ability to create something new by rethinking, recombining and reconfiguring the old.

While creativity's historical link to intentionality and to the genius artist is unsurprising, it's equally true that art and creativity have changed dramatically in the past two centuries, as the many companies looking to hire creative people on LinkedIn shows. Retaining novelty as part of creativity means, therefore, that we must rethink the assumption that a creator's successful separation from the world is a prerequisite of creating something new. Simply put, creativity must be explained without relying on creators transcending their own history and culture.

American Hungarian Psychologist Mihaly Csikszentmihalyi (2014) uses a systems theory approach to creativity to provide an answer to the question of novelty in today's world, by examining the role that culture, society and individual background have on sparking creativity. He begins

[3] George Becker maintains that this mystical aspect is precisely what still connects modern with classical notions of the creative genius: "While the modern conception of genius is quite different from the classical use of the term, its indebtedness to antiquity is apparent in the retention of a markedly mystical component. The semireligious quality surrounding the notion of genius constitutes a cornerstone in the association of genius with madness" (Becker 1978, p. 21).

by reminding us that "[W]e cannot study creativity by isolating individuals and their works from the social and historical milieu in which their actions are carried out" (Csikszentmihalyi 2014, p. 47). The reason for this is related to the forces shaping the individual's ability to act, such as, for example, their education. These forces not only provide a certain direction but also define the boundaries that an individual encounters when introducing something new to the world; the individual does not define novelty on their own, but depends on others, who will ultimately judge any output as original or not.

For Csikszentmihalyi creativity is shaped by three specific forces. The first one is what he calls "a set of social institutions, or field, that selects from the variations produced by individuals those that are worth preserving" (Csikszentmihalyi, p. 47). This field or set of institutions sets in a way the rules that a society uses to define creativity. This refers, for instance, to the role that a film award like the Oscars plays in guiding the public about the merits of the films produced in a particular year. Next to these institutions, you have "a stable cultural domain that will preserve and transmit the selected new ideas or forms to the following generations" (Csikszentmihalyi, p. 47). The film industry, the music industry and, naturally, the art industry are all stable domains in the sense that they provide the right context to present and preserve a creative output to the public. They provide the right space for the public to encounter a creative output. The existence of theatres, archives and film museums is needed for the film industry to have permanence. The right space refers as well to a space that supports the process of deterritorialization and territorialization, as explained earlier. Lastly, Csikszentmihalyi argues the third force is "the individual, who brings about some change in the domain, a change that the field will consider to be creative" (Csikszentmihalyi, p. 48). To remain with the examples from the film industry, the introduction of sound was the result of certain individuals who challenged the canon of the time that saw film as a purely visual medium, which needed to be preserved as such (Fig. 2.1).

Csikszentmihalyi's systems approach to creativity doesn't do away with the individual but rather qualifies their role in a way not dissimilar to Latour's network approach. The creator, for both Latour and Csikszentmihalyi, experiments with materials that are embedded within a

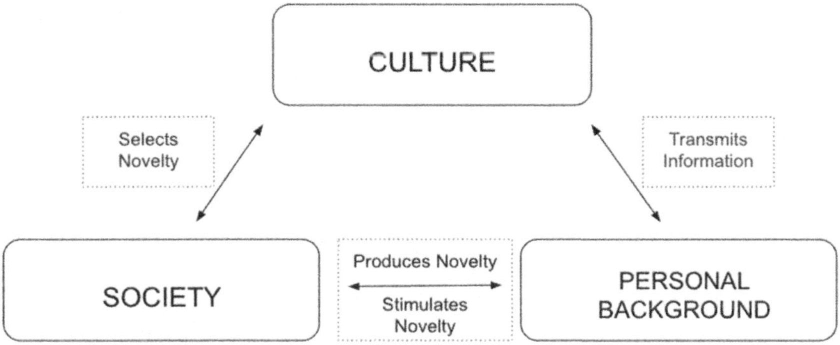

Fig. 2.1 Diagram of the systems approach to creativity, relating culture, society and persona background, based on Mihaly Csikszentmihalyi's (2014) model

historic and socio-cultural context.[4] In Latour, this refers to the materials, tools and technologies that are always part of pre-existing networks that give them a role and a meaning that a creator will follow or challenge. These networks, to restate, are inhabited by human and non-human actors that determine their output. This inseparability between creators and their milieu allows me to bring ANT close to this systems approach to creativity. Novelty is core to both views and is the result of actors being able to collaborate imaginatively, as in being able to reimagine existing networks and propose new ones. It's also the result of those actors being able to collaborate autonomously, that is, without the need to follow a predefined path or to arrive at a predetermined destination.

Digital artist and researcher Lev Manovich argues along these lines that imagination, novelty and autonomy are essential to creativity but are not the whole story. He notices that for creativity to be linked to a specific context, it must also be worthwhile or useful. He notices that making something novel "does not automatically make something culturally or socially interesting or significant" (Manovich 2023b, p. 2). Manovich's addition is not inconsequential. It brings the notion of novelty even closer to the idea of territorialization, which emphasizes impact, manifested on

[4] A similar view can be found from neuroengineering professor Paul Verschure, who also sees at the problem of creativity as emerging from the interaction between an individual and its environment, arguing that creativity results "from the interaction between agents and their environment, and places creativity in the context of the necessary role of discovery and exploration in all processes underlying life" (Verschure 2018, p. 2).

the way in which creativity pushes actors to rethink and reconfigure existing networks. By stating that novelty must be useful or worthwhile Manovich reminds us that while shock, and the challenging of old ideas, is essential to the public-work encounter, it's not sufficient for it to be impactful. Shock (deterritorialization) is but the first step towards a reconfiguration of a network, the door towards new ways of looking at things. Yet, it's through (re)territorialization that novelty becomes truly actualized, truly a part of people's lives. Experience, inspiration and education provide the creator(s) with the tools needed to understand the networks they are a part of, and creative practices outline novel to reconfigure them.

When it comes to the role of AI, what makes the question about its impact meaningful is not whether one can confidently state that AI will replace human talent, but whether AI systems can become part of the creative networks that are today responsible for the creation of films, music, games, books and of course art. Going back to the example of the *Portrait of Belamy*, "many actors were involved: the programmers of the original algorithmic architecture, the coders who updated and adapted it, the artists who marketed and sold it, and the algorithmic system itself which output the final result" (Moruzzi 2022, p. 15). Furthermore, none of these actors worked in isolation, but always as part of a "dynamic of relations with a network of other actors and contextual factors" (Moruzzi, p. 15). If creativity is always networked and all actors have a concrete role within these networks, then to assess whether AI was impactful in the making of the *Portrait of Belamy* one must know, staying with Moruzzi, how agency is "distributed in the network of actors who contribute to the [creative practices] in question" (p. 15).

The systems' approach to creativity highlighted the importance of external factors in enabling or hindering creativity. Emphasizing the role of external factors, such as environment and culture, makes context fundamental to assess the impact of AI systems on creativity today. Equally important is thinking about the type of technological developments that are likely to benefit or hinder future creativity. A series of relevant questions capture this conclusion: what is the politico-economic reality that gave birth to today's AI? What are the beliefs and promises informing AI narratives within that reality? And, how does the emergence of AI systems support or challenge today's creative networks, both inside and outside the artworld?

The Economy at the Dawn of AI: Concentration, Financialization and Wage Stagnation

This section addresses the question of context, beginning from an economic point of view. A clear picture of the macroeconomic context, of the figures and predictions that are used to appeal to firms and investors, is core to understanding the effect of today's AI narratives. With the context laid out, the text will then discuss in greater detail the type of narrative that has taken shape on the societal impact of AI, since the introduction of LLMs or transformer-based models like ChatGPT.

My intention will not be to present a historical account of the development of AI systems in the past century, for which comprehensive research already exists.[5] The purpose of my analysis is, first, to outline the economic forces that have driven and will drive the development of AI systems in the coming decade. Second, to show how such forces shape the dominant narrative behind the predictions on the impact of AI in the overall economy, and within specific industries. This text will argue three particular economic forces have driven and will continue to drive the development of AI systems, mainly but not exclusively, in developed economies: increased market concentration, financialization of the economy and wage stagnation.

"Competition is for losers", stated American billionaire Peter Thiel in the *Wall Street Journal* in 2014. Despite being over a decade old, his words capture the economic trajectory followed by the developed world for the past 40 years. In 2023 investment and asset managers BlackRock, Vanguard and State Street became the largest shareholders in 90% of firms listed in the NYSE; BlackRock manages ten trillion in investments, Vanguard eight trillion and State Street four trillion (adding up to almost the entire US GDP in 2021) (Varoufakis 2023, p. 111). When so much equity sits in the hands of so few, market competition becomes a fiction. While consumers may experience a variety of brands to choose from, the reality is that many of such brands are likely to be owned by the same shareholders and often by the same corporation. Unilever, to name a case in point, owns brands like Axe, Dove and Rexona, which seemingly compete across a variety of personal care product categories. It also owns both Ben & Jerry's and Magnum ice-cream. The situation is such that FTC

[5] For such an account I would recommend reading Mateo Pasquinelli's (2023) *The Eye of the Master: A Social History of Artificial Intelligence*.

chair Lina Khan stated that the decline in competition is so consistent across markets that it seems more and more like a systemic feature of the American economy (Doctorow and Giblin 2022, p. 6). Moreover, higher concentration is neither recent, nor confined to business ownership: in the US, from 1935 to 1989 the number of small farms declined from 6.8 million to under 2.1 million (while the population roughly doubled) (Korten 2001, p. 208).

Such concentration increases the effective power that corporations have in dictating the terms under which they operate. In other words, it allows business to hold sway over institutions potentially coercing them to act on their behalf, including pressuring a country's legislative branch or supranational institutions like the European parliament or the World Bank. As Marxist geographer David Harvey puts it, the visible hand of multinational corporations has played a much bigger role in the uneven development that we see in the world today, than the actual hidden hand of market competition (Harvey 2006, p. 100). When one or only a few firms control a sizable part of the market, they hinder competition and, along with it, all the positive aspects that people expect from such competition: lower prices, innovative products, greater choice, etc.

The second economic force at the centre of capitalist development in the past four decades is financialization. In the year 2000 the world's total income was 70 trillion USD, of which an approximated 50 trillion were held in financial assets. By 2007 total income had risen to 75 trillion, while the global financial market had risen to 750 trillion (Varoufakis 2023, p. 40). Important to add is that such staggering growth of the financial economy didn't mean that the average financial wealth of most people grew simultaneously or proportionately. Most financial wealth followed the same concentration path, remaining in the hands of the highest earners. In the US 50% of all public stocks are owned by the wealthiest 1% (Caporal 2024).[6]

Perhaps the most direct way in which asset concentration is kept in check is through wage growth. Wage growth is the mechanism that ensures that talent is spread across competing businesses and that financialization results in everyone having greater access to things like credit, as well as stocks, next to a host of other financial options. Wage growth was, not surprisingly, at the heart of the industrial development of today's

[6] In the UK, for instance, only 10% of all bank lending went to non-financial firms, while the rest supported real estate and financial assets (Mazzucato 2021, p. 16).

developed economies. Economist Branko Milanovic argues that after the 1820s the West had been consistently wealthier than any other part of the world, in large part because by the middle of the nineteenth century, even members of the working class in Western countries were better off than their global peers (Milanovic 2020, pp. 5, 6). Sadly, he continues, "that period is now coming to an end" (p. 5). In the US, working-class earnings remain on average below their 1974 levels (Varoufakis 2023, p. 46). In fact, the US minimum wage hasn't changed since 2009, remaining stuck at 7.25 USD an hour. Similarly, UK real wages have barely changed since their 2008 levels (Andrews and Croal 2023). Beyond the US and the UK, real median wages in OECD countries between 1995 and 2013 grew annually at a meagre 0.8% while productivity grew twice as fast, at an annual rate of 1.5% (Mazzucato 2021, p. 11). The case of Japan's economic and wage stagnation is particularly eye-watering, with real wages barely changing since the 1990s (Kubo 2022, p. 1). Wage stagnation, the third economic force, is consistent with an economy that is increasingly less competitive and more concentrated. It's also consistent with higher levels of inequality, which is why CEO pay has not only not stagnated but increased nearly 1000% in the US in the past 50 years (Doctorow and Giblin 2022, p. 6).

Concentration, financialization and wage stagnation are all factors consistent with the reality of today's AI firms: systems created by a handful of very large US firms with the ability to undertake the heavy investments needed and with the right incentive to do them, given that, if successful, this will all but guarantee them a dominant position in the high-tech market. The goals, researchers Luitse and Denkena (2021) claim about OpenAI, are to attempt to create a rentier market. This attempt to have a rentier's position is in line with the model followed by the established Big Tech giants of today (e.g. Uber, Airbnb, Netflix, Meta, etc.), where growth was always prioritized over profitability. Growth means, in this context, facilitating the mass adoption of their platforms and services, enabling them to capture an audience. All of this is made possible by the current "unequal distribution of large-scale computing resources" (Luitse and Denkena, p. 10). Only in a concentrated economy with stagnated wages can such a risky growth strategy be worth pursuing. For it to work, investors must be fully confident that a firm will be able to increase prices at will, once it has successfully captured most, if not all, of the market it operates in. Moreover, continue Luitse and Denkena, this strategy explains too OpenAI's relationship to Microsoft, which gives the latter an exclusive licence to OpenAI's underlying code and with it the unique ability to modify, configure or embed it into their overall cloud computing infrastructure, which caters to commercial customers (Hao 2020), as well as to their consumer products, which are used by hundreds of millions across the globe (Langston 2021).

However, US companies are not the only relevant players in the AI domain. China is an equally important player whose trajectory in the past four decades has been very different. It has not been shaped by the concentration, financialization and wage stagnation seen during the same period in the developed West. In fact, any mention of China must begin acknowledging the economic miracle that has characterized the country's development in the past four decades. In 2010 China marked an incredible milestone, having lifted more than 700 million rural Chinese out of poverty since the early 1980s (Luo and Xie 2020, p. 1). By 2019 China accounted for 19% of the world's economic output (Luo et al.). Given this neck-breaking pace of growth there is no doubt that the past decades in China can be characterized as anything, except from stagnation. Branco Milanovic (2020) argues in this respect that were China to continue outpacing the US economy by "two to three percentage points of per capita income growth every year, the average income gap between the two countries (in 2021 4,7 to 1) will take about two generations to close" (p. 6).

Yet, while the US and China may have followed very different paths in the past four decades their economies do share a striking similarity in one sense: inequality. According to Luo et al. (2020) the Gini of income inequality in China as a whole increased from 0.381 in 1988 to 0.462 in 1995, and then to 0.471 in 2002 and 0.490 in 2007 (up to 0.557 in 2015) (pp. 1–9). The authors add that in 2009 the "per capita household income in urban areas was over 2.5 times that of rural households in the real terms" (p. 3). The issue of inequality is not accidental, but central to the trajectory of Chinese development. For comparison Milanovic (2021) argues that in a span going from the mid-1980s to 2013 the Gini of the US increased by four points, while that of China increased by 20 points (Milanovic 2021, p. 102), which leads to the, perhaps surprising, fact that the capital income of the top 1% in both China and the US is strikingly similar (Milanovic, p. 104).

The fact that China is today, next to the US, a leader in the development of AI and other technologies may seem counterintuitive for some. We often hear that Chinese economic growth has been mainly based on the production of low-tech goods, exemplified by the success of companies like Shein or Temu. This is a wrong assumption to make as the reality is that China has, on the contrary, focused on high-tech manufacturing: high-tech offshoring increased from around 14% in the 1990s to 18% by 2006, while offshoring in low-tech industries has remained stable at 8% (Milanovic, p. 152).

What does this broad macro perspective tell us? It tells us that AI has come to life in an age of profound economic inequality. This means that its adoption, use and potential benefits are likely to be just as unequal. Today's economic news about AI becoming the driver of an upcoming productivity revolution should be read with that context in mind. Goldman Sachs (2024) estimated that AI systems could raise global GDP by 7% (or seven trillion USD) and lift productivity growth by 1.5 percentage points over a ten-year period and two-thirds of the occupations would be partially automated.

The consultancy giant McKinsey claimed that business cases related to Gen AI alone would deliver between 2.6 and 4.4 trillion of a whopping 17.7 trillion USD, which they estimate as the resulting value of all business uses of AI (Chui et al. 2024, p. 9). As a reference, the authors mention, the annual GDP of the UK in 2021 was 3.1 trillion USD. Similarly positive scenarios are also being painted about the impact of AI in the Chinese economy, where it is estimated that AI will result in 600 billion USD of annual economic value (for comparison, Shanghai's GDP is 680 billion).

Differences do begin to emerge when we take a closer look at the expected business cases for AI in China and the West. McKinsey's report claims that the biggest beneficiaries of AI in China will be the automotive, transportation and logistics sectors, which are expected to collectively contribute around 64% of the total $600 billion opportunity (Shen et al. 2022). The rest of the benefits McKinsey concludes are expected to fall on manufacturing (around 19%), enterprise software (13%) and healthcare and life sciences (4%). In the developed West the story is markedly different, with 75% of the value of Gen AI expected to fall across only four areas: customer operations, marketing and sales, software engineering and R&D (Chui et al., p. 11).

Such high hopes in the marketing and sales industry explain, for instance, the partnership between technology titan Nvidia, whose GPUs are essential to Gen AI, and the world's largest advertising agency WPP (2023). A similar partnership between the third largest advertising and media network, Publicis Groupe and Microsoft, further exemplifies the vested hope in the transformative potential of Gen AI in marketing

(Publicis Groupe 2024). However, the hype is not confined to the big fish in the industry. Research agency Forrester claims that 91% of creative agencies in the US already use or are exploring Gen AI (Baar 2024).

Focus on these sectors does suggest an important difference in the expectation for AI systems in China, in comparison to the West. Gen AI and its uses, for example, in AI-Art, are not unknown to Chinese companies. Baidu CEO Robin Li asserted, for instance, that their company's ERNIE Bot is better than GPT-4 at generating Chinese poetry in the style of the Tang Dynasty, which shows that the fascination with Gen AI is not exclusive to the West's gaze (Triolo and Schaefer 2024). Moreover, clients of the ERNIE bot include key enterprise users like Samsung China, Lenovo and Honor in addition to over 26,000 other enterprise users, most of them local. Similarly, the same authors claim, Chinese company Alibaba claims its own bot QWEN has over 90,000 enterprise users, again mainly local.

One important reason explaining the relatively minor role of Gen AI in China relates to the current restrictions on non-Chinese GPUs, which make AI developers in that country more reliable, at least in the short term, on open-source models.[7] Another reason may be purely economic in nature, and it would mean that Chinese companies don't see a major role for Gen AI, at least in the short term, outside of the customer relations business case, which explains the development of the ERNIE and QWEN bots. Very recent developments may, however, challenge this story. The LLM DeepSeek was launched as an open-source model in late 2024, grabbing headlines due to its parity with the latest ChatGPT versions, albeit with a much lower price tag. It's too early to tell how such developments may change the speed of adoption of LLMs soon, but it's not farfetched to assume that its substantially lower price and efficient use of computer may accelerate its adoption in the Global South.

Given this tsunami of positive economic predictions, it's fair to ask, how will these benefits actually come about? For McKinsey the answer is productivity. Bringing back to mind their forecasted \$2.6 trillion to \$4.4 trillion of expected annual revenue, they argue that current Gen AI and other technologies have the potential to automate work activities that

[7] GPUs power virtually all LLMs today, and the world leader in their manufacturing is Nvidia: the Nvidia A100, H100, or newer G200 or AMD's advanced GPUs in the cloud via Infrastructure-as-a-Service (IaaS) channels, all need to be imported. Not surprisingly Nvidia has seen its stock rise close to 2700% in the past five years.

absorb 60 to 70% of employees' time today (Chui et al. 2024). This, they add, is an upwardly revised forecast from an initial prediction that AI technologies would automate up to 50% or employees' time. The reason for this update, they continue "is largely due to Generative AI's increased ability to understand natural language, which is required for work activities that account for 25 percent of total work time. Thus, Generative AI has more impact on knowledge work associated with occupations that have higher wages and educational requirements than on other types of work" (Chui et al.).

Freeing up 60 to 70% of a worker's daily tasks sounds truly revolutionary. For an office worker this could potentially mean no more time spent writing or responding to emails, substantially less meetings, less or no time doing or analysing research, less or no time dedicated to doing reports, the sky's the limit, or is it? What type of across-the-board activities does McKinsey refer to here? Within marketing and sales, they state that "Generative AI could significantly reduce the time required for ideation and content drafting, saving valuable time and effort … Mass email campaigns can be instantly translated into as many languages as needed, with different imagery and messaging depending on the audience" (Chui et al.). No real depth is provided on how time spent on ideation would be saved without sacrificing quality. It's difficult to imagine how, for instance, an AI system would take an ad created in English for the US market, translate it to Vietnamese and visually adapt it to that market. As someone working in the industry this is a literal example of one of the toughest problems faced by global brands: to create a communications strategy that is both consistent and relevant to the needs of consumers in local markets.[8]

It's important to highlight that McKinsey's claims of increased productivity resonate with the view of AI as a tool created to lighten work, which is something few people would argue against. Economists Acemoglu and Johnson (2023) provide a somewhat critical view of the lightening of work argument. They see it as part of what they call the productivity bandwagon theory, which, simply put, is the belief that technological development is always beneficial to workers and should always be welcomed with open arms (Acemoglu and Johnson 2023, p. 5). A case in point is the

[8] While still vague in what it entails, McKinsey does add that "Generative AI's ability to produce content with varying specifications could increase customer value, attraction, conversion, and retention over a lifetime and at a scale beyond what is currently possible through traditional techniques" (Chui et al. 2024).

Techno-Optimist manifesto by venture capitalist Mark Andreesen, who in 2023 wrote "[w]e believe a market sets wages as function of the marginal productivity of the worker. Therefore technology—which raises productivity—drives wages up, not down. This is perhaps the most counterintuitive idea in all of Economics, but it's true, and we have 300 years of history that prove it" (Acemoglu and Johnson, p. xii). Acemoglu and Johnson bluntly state that Andreesen's understanding of history seems to be completely flawed, adding that in the past 1000 years of history there is no evidence that remotely suggests the existence of an automatic mechanism that ensures that ordinary people benefit from technological improvements. Andreesen's claim is ideological through and through and can only result from cherry-picking very particular instances. It ignores that many new technologies have negatively impacted the quality of work that they make available.

In short, their main critique of the productivity bandwagon is twofold. They claim primarily that it ignores the costs that even a short-term disruption generates. Secondly, and in my view more importantly, given the economic context described earlier, it fails to explain how workers would be the main economic beneficiaries of firms adopting AI (Acemoglu and Johnson, p. 7). Given today's state of inequality, due to increased market concentration and the wage stagnation that results from it, one must be at least somewhat sceptical of the idea that most economic benefits will be enjoyed by the workers.

Furthermore, Spencer (2024) raises a crucial point in Acemoglu and Johnson's approach. He argues their research is focused on "preserving work rather than on curtailing it. This is to suggest that people are mainly interested in maintaining their work lives and ignore their interests and needs in securing more time away from work" (Spencer 2024, p. 1). Spencer is right in pointing out that if the predicted productivity gains come to fruition, there is no reason why such gains would be used by workers to increase their workload. He argues instead that productivity gains will allow workers to enjoy a better quality of life, because they can work less without sacrificing any income. If McKinsey is right and workers may find themselves being able to free up 60 to 70% of their working day, why would this not lead to a decrease in the amount of overall time worked? This is not even a novel idea. During the first half of the twentieth century Nobel laureate John Maynard Keynes already expected that productivity gains would mean that by the year 2030 workers would enjoy a 15-hour working week without sacrificing quality of life.

What Spencer makes evident is the ideology at work behind the lightening of work argument. The idea that people would use any spare time to do more work makes sense only in a world where work remains the main way in which people find meaning in their lives. While there is some truth to the fact that people do work expecting more than just a pay cheque, it's also true that work is not the only way in which meaning is found. Leisure is much more than simply rest. He reminds us, "leisure is also about engaging in all sorts of activities, from hobbies and sport to the exploration of interests that are fulfilling in and of themselves; many of which are creative (e.g. writing, painting, sculpting, wood working, dancing, etc.)" (Spencer, p. 7).[9]

Economic hardship, however, means that Spencer's argument, as interesting as it may be, generates a lesser sense of urgency than the very practical concern that AI systems will simply mean either fewer jobs or lower-quality jobs in the near future. Acemoglu and Johnson (2023) are, for instance, concerned that much AI technology is being used for what they term "so-so" automation. They mean with this that AI adoption often means automating human labour without any large (positive) productivity effect (p. 19). To make their point, they discuss the appearance of self-service checkouts at retail stores, which, they argue, displace rather than automate work; the technology doesn't replace cashiers but transforms consumers themselves into cashiers. Another example is Amazon warehouses, which use AI to monitor work and increase work intensity but are detrimental to the workers themselves. In Amazon's case, increased productivity has a negative effect on workers, which, one may argue, is not something that should normalize as a society.

Lastly, researchers Deck (2022) and Roose (2022) have also shown that members of the artistic community share the concern that Gen AI will simply end up taking away jobs from artists. It's not that artists and creators think that some embodied AI will replace the human creator, but rather that the way in which AI companies use data, belonging to past and current creators, to train their systems is highly problematic. For instance, Brewer et al. (2024) note that creators critical of Gen AI have accused their mother companies of theft "by scraping their artwork from the internet and using it in image-generating algorithms without obtaining

[9] Spencer does remain sceptical of the system's ability to see the value of leisure. For him "any radical redirection of AI towards the lightening of work will require fundamental change in the way that the economy is owned and governed" (Spencer 2024, p. 11).

consent from, crediting, or compensating the original artists" (p. 77). Along these lines the technology magazine *The Verge* reported that "a group of artists has filed a lawsuit against AI image generator companies—as has Getty Images, a leading stock image provider" (Vincent 2023).

While perhaps incomplete, this brief picture of the economic context in which AI systems have dawned shows how rosy predictions about economic growth live side by side a multitude of justifiable concerns that go, from the uneven distribution of rewards, job automation and displacement, all the way to outright fears and accusations of theft. The sceptic may reply that such contradictions are inherent to most innovations, and we shouldn't be too surprised by them. This will no doubt ring true in certain circles, but in reality, it's anything but obvious how such coexistence is possible. After all, why aren't most creators concerned about their property rights? Or why would artists like Jason Allen or the Obvious collective be so enthusiastic about the incorporation of AI systems in their work? And how about the myriads of less well-known copywriters, filmmakers and music producers, among many others, who are likely to raise the same type of concerns around job replacement, job displacement and loss of intellectual property rights?

Going beyond the economic figures and predictions presented so far is necessary, in order to make sense of this mixed bag of benefits and detriments discussed. A second layer of analysis is in order. To do so the text will turn towards a broader, less economically focused, perspective, in order to fully grasp how such apparent contradictions can coexist. From this vantage point a red thread will emerge, which is needed to fully understand the impact of AI on creativity and provide a final answer to the question: can AI be creative?

Neoliberalism's Political Economy and the Dawn of the Creative Class

In *New Spirit of capitalism* sociologists Boltanski and Chiapello show how the adoption of organizational changes introduced in the late 1970s helped shape the economic context that we see today.[10] Their ideas show how a universal narrative focused on high growth and high productivity can coexist with a context of market concentration, financialization and

[10] I will focus here only on some of the key ideas presented by the authors at the Conference of Europeanists in 2002, based on their larger *The New Spirit of capitalism*.

stagnation. More importantly, their ideas help us understand how a new generation of artists or creators, along with their creative networks, became part of the modern workplace.

Neoliberalism, argue Boltanski and Chiapello, is the ideological underpinning that became the dominant economic view that persists till this day.[11] Neoliberalism appeared as a reviving spirit to the ailments of capitalism in the 1970s. Rather than a continuation of post-war capitalism, focused on centralized planning and continuous state intervention, Neoliberalism appeared, in contrast, as a rekindling of free markets that would disarm the critical anti-capitalist forces that were brewing at the time.[12] The early 1970s witnessed what was then called the *oil crisis*. This crisis resulted from an oil embargo by the OPEC cartel that generated an explosive fourfold increase in the price of oil during that decade.[13] This situation, not surprisingly, had a very negative impact on economic growth, at a time where slowing economic growth was already a concern. Rather than simply blaming the outside forces responsible for the embargo or the overall reliance on oil, Neoliberalism interpreted the crisis as a failure of the prevailing organizational models and proposed solutions intended to reinvigorate people's trust in capitalism (Boltanski and Chiapello 2002, p. 2).

They argue, one of the key issues in the latter half of the 1970s was deteriorating worker conditions. Neoliberalism blamed the prevailing organizational model: the Fordist model, defined by factory lines and obedient dedicated workers. Neoliberalism derided this model, seeing in its traditional forms of authority, based on strict hierarchies, the main culprit for the lack of worker motivation and low productivity growth. The demand for autonomy became, hence, an acknowledged concern, and with it the recommendation that "advantages that had hitherto been restricted to executives (autonomous teams, flexible schedules, bonuses, efficiency-related salaries, etc.) were generalised to all categories of management" (Boltanski and Chiapello, p. 18).

[11] They are far from alone in this designation as the term is fairly common among economists and political scientists today.

[12] In this regard the authors state that "In fact, it is probably capitalism's amazing ability to survive by endogenizing of some of the criticisms it faces that has helped in recent times to disarm the forces of anticapitalism, giving way to a triumphant version of capitalism" (Boltanski and Chiapello 2002, p. 1).

[13] The price of oil went from less than 20USD a barrel in 1972 to 100USD by the 1980s after the Iranian revolution.

Along these lines, around 1975 shareholders and company leadership reacted to the lower profits following the oil crisis, by adopting a new strategy that looked to address an array of critical social demands concerned with a variety of forms of workplace oppression: "factory discipline, the massification of society, standardisation and pervasive commodification" were derided, making way for the vindication of "an ideal of liberation and/or of individual autonomy, singularity and authenticity" (p. 16). At the organizational level, challenging hierarchies resulted in rethinking the centralized decision-making models that came along with it. The answer to inflexible hierarchies included an openness to break down "large integrated companies into a series of small units that were connected through a network of contracts (temporary work, subcontracting, outsourcing activities that did not belong to the company's core business, etc.)" (p. 18).

This new spirit envisioned nimble, fast-paced workplaces, where autonomous workers would find greater motivation as well as greater opportunities to engage with multiple employers instead of staying attached to a single firm. This was the first step in the direction of a new type of employee-entrepreneur, or freelancer, which also led to the mandatory personal branding that we see millions display effortlessly on their LinkedIn profiles today. More broadly, Neoliberalism's proposal can be summed up in three dimensions: excitement for the future, income security and a sense of justice or fairness (p. 3). Excitement for the future was the response to a 1970s' economic system that seemed at a standstill and unable to deliver on its promise for a better life. It meant, in turn, reinterpreting capitalism as a system that not only would give people a wage, but also help them blossom, find their passion and, in some cases, become their own boss (pp. 3, 7). This newfound excitement for work carried with it a natural rejection of the divide between leisure and work. The reason being that a worker who is following their passion should be able to dedicate as much time to it as possible, not merely a fixed number of hours on a predetermined schedule during the week. Security, the second dimension, meant emphasizing to workers that a reinvigoration of the system would improve their economic prospects, but also that their children's financial success depended on it. Addressing the system's issues was therefore not intended as a tweak or reform, but as a long-lasting and fundamental change that would impact generations to come. Lastly, a sense of justice or fairness refers to rethinking work as not only a form of self-development, but also as a form of recognition (merit) and a contribution to the common good.

This meant putting meritocracy and workplace competition front and centre of Neoliberalism's agenda.

How do these changes impact the way in which people relate and collaborate? Less hierarchical structures, openness to continuous change and decentralized decision-making transforms how information flows within a company as well as the role of both workers and managers. A new model of the firm emerges as a result.[14] One that emphasizes autonomy and meritocracy, where every worker and mid-manager becomes a responsible stakeholder rather than a follower of instructions. The ideal organization would allow for collaboration and teams to emerge organically and define the best ways to deliver an output while constantly adapting to changing economic circumstances.

The astute reader may see in these changes that the proposed organizational changes ultimately transformed the slow-moving bureaucratic firm with its top-down decision-making process into a network. Within this new idea of the firm, Neoliberalism proposes too, a new set of actors, that is, a new set of roles for the humans that take part in such networks: the worker-entrepreneur, the shareholder-manager, the founder-CEO and the consumer-entrepreneur (or prosumer). With these new roles, new relationships emerge, allowing for ideas to flow within the firm, but also to come in from the outside. When networks become an organizational principle, the firm is no longer a closed structure. Openness means that a firm gains the ability to connect with other firms and other external actors. This means that relations with contractors, freelancers and other firms should no longer be the exception but the rule (p. 22). It also means that different teams within a firm can function as a network within a network, given the higher degree of autonomy and decentralization championed by the new spirit. The hope of this newfound autonomy and rekindled motivation was that it would help spark innovation, while getting rid of costly hierarchies and slow, inflexible processes (p. 22).

[14] "This analysis has led us to conclude that a new representation of the firm has emerged, featuring an organisation that is very flexible; organised by projects; works in a network; features few hierarchical levels; where a logic of transversal flows has replaced a more hierarchical one, etc. This new representation contrasts specifically with a former representation of the firm, one that had focused on an organisation which is hierarchical, integrated and geared towards the internal realisation of activities (vertical integration). This had been a dominant form during the 1960s, praised at the time but subsequently decried (by the 1990s authors) for its excessive "bureaucracy" " (Boltanski and Chiapello, p. 4).

There are, to be sure, a plethora of criticisms that can be made regarding the purported benefits of such changes. Scepticism about its practical implementation during the following four decades is also warranted. My interest in sparingly exploring some of the main ideas of the new spirit is not to deliver a defence of Neoliberalism. The purpose of surveying Boltanski and Chiapello's work is to see how elements like autonomy, productivity, decentralization, flexibility, innovation and meritocracy, all come together to become part of a single narrative. They are used to interpret economic facts, transforming cold predictions about economic growth into exciting personal opportunities, while safely dismissing the financial pressure that a flexible job market puts on workers. Regardless of the criticism, decentralization, autonomy and a greater flow of ideas did open the door for a new type of workplace collaboration to emerge. The network, it turns out, allowed for creative practices, previously seen as incompatible with the workplace, to become essential to the neoliberal firm.

To understand how this process took place the text turns to American sociologist Richard Florida and his ideas on what he calls the *Creative Class*. In short, Florida's concept of the Creative Class uses economic and cultural statistics to show how, at the turn of the century, creativity became the red thread that explained the growth of a range of industries, including advertising, game design, industrial design and architecture, among many others.[15] While all these economic sectors produce very different things (goods, services or *experiences*), Florida argues that they all have one thing in common: creativity as the core driver of their economic value.[16]

The Unexpected Rise of the Creative Class

We often hear that we live in an interconnected world, as part of a globalized economy. While familiar, this often feels quite distant from our day-to-day reality. We commonly assume that such statements refer mainly to

[15] Florida's Creative Economy includes research institutes, universities and think tanks.

[16] The "Experiential Economy" is a related concept, developed by Pine and Gilmore (1999), that is worthwhile to keep in mind as one of the ways in which free market narratives have incorporated the notion of creativity as a natural development of capitalism. In short, the authors argue capitalism has reached a stage in which companies should no longer follow the logic of commoditization, which dictates lower marginal costs as the goal of successful production processes, instead replacing it with the notion of higher marginal value, resulting from a more intensive use of creative labour.

political and economic relationships between countries or multinational corporations. This perception often misses Boltanski and Chiapello's point on Neoliberalism's recipe to rethink organizational structures, based on meritocracy, productivity and autonomy. Such a recipe has been implemented for over four decades in many countries, making it a lived reality for billions around the world. Most office workers today are quite familiar with firms of all sizes using terms like autonomy, productivity and meritocracy as part of their corporate jargon, especially when describing the relationship with their employees. At the level of the individual, globalization is certainly more than jargon. It means, among other things, that remote teams can be put together and that human actors within those teams can come from very different backgrounds and disciplines. Decentralized decision-making and greater autonomy mean that such teams can organize themselves in the way they deem fit, without waiting for a central authority to define their roles. In the developed West this has resulted in a pluralistic and multicultural workplace, where millions of office workers are part of teams made up of people from different ethnicities and different cultural and educational backgrounds. Flatter organizational structures and multidisciplinary, multicultural teams open the door to ways of working that were unlikely in more centralized and hierarchical forms of organization. In flatter structures, ideas and processes cannot simply be imposed without at least some degree of justification. Trust among members is central to a team's proper functioning, and dialogue and consensus are needed in order for alignment to be reached about the standards and expectations shaping their collaboration. These changes also allowed for a particular type of network, a creative network to, for the first time, find a natural place inside a capitalist firm.

Whatever advantages Neoliberalism derives from such organizational changes, like the hope that the products and services made will deliver a higher value to consumers, and hence can be sold at a higher price, there is in any case no straightforward connection between this mode of organization and greater efficiency. What the network does enable is for old processes and ideas to be challenged, while new ideas and new processes are trialled and tested. In other words, Florida concludes, these larger organizational changes brought forward by Neoliberalism allow creativity to become a fundamental part of a system of production that emphasizes value creation over cost reduction. It's this conclusion that ignites Florida's interest in the role that creativity plays in today's economy. Creativity, he states, "is now the decisive source of competitive advantage. In virtually every industry, from automobiles to fashion, food products, and information technology itself, the winners in the long run are those who can create and keep creating" (Florida 2004, p. 5).[17] What makes creativity prevalent among very different sectors of the economy, Florida continues, is the need that firms in those sectors have to "revise and enhance every product, process and activity imaginable, and fit them together in new ways" (Florida, p. 5). Stated differently, the need to reconfigure existing products, rethink problems faced by consumers and explore new ideas, is what makes the Creative Class central to the system shaped by Neoliberalism.[18]

Yet, these changes affect not only the flows that take place inside a firm, but consistent with Boltanski and Chiapello open them up to external ideas, including those coming from "artistic and cultural creativity" (p. 5). In practice, we can see this happening even in the legacy of Cybernetics, which despite going out of fashion in the late 1970s lives on in fields such as Control Theory and Complex Systems Studies, Interaction Design and Design Thinking (Pieters and Winiger 2016). It can likewise be seen in "the development of first generation assisted creation systems in the 1980s: Photoshop, AutoCAD, Pro-Tools, Word and many more". This flow of ideas external to the firm only multiplies as the Creative Class sets in. Autocorrect was invented in 1991 and autotune, invented in 1998, transforms how music is made (Pieters and Winiger). The impact of any of these systems is hard to measure, because it's not simply a matter of increasing a worker's productivity or decreasing a firm's costs. Its impact has also to do with their ability to allow experts to shift their attention to more demanding or higher-level issues, while lowering the bar for non-experts. In this sense, being open to external ideas allows firms to benefit from the value created by external creative networks, in turn empowering and improving their own internal networks.

Networks, with their ability to connect different actors, whose role can change and adapt are precisely the type of structure needed for people and ideas coming from different disciplines to find in those differences a space

[17] For Florida the creative economy is already fairly large: including scientific research and development, high-tech industries, new-media communications, advertisement, traditional bohemian circles, etc., to name but a few concrete examples.

[18] Florida's Creative Class should not be equated with the service sectors of the economy. He distances from the Marxist concept of immaterial labour, which Hardt and Negri (2000) define as "labour that produces an immaterial good, such as a service, a cultural product, knowledge, or communication" (p. 290).

of collaboration rather than a threat. The Creative Class depends on workers who can generate new ideas and adopt new technologies, and includes workers within sectors like music, entertainment, design, architecture and the arts, but also workers in less obvious sectors like science, engineering and education.[19]

Reconciling a single notion of creativity with the many types of products and services produced across various economic sectors can justifiably raise some questions. However, it's not at all unusual to refer to a film, a book or a sculpture, as examples of creativity, even if their material components, function and meaning are clearly distinct. Likewise, an architect, a musician and a video game designer will by no means create similar outputs, yet they are all part of the Creative Class. What this tells us is that "creativity is multidimensional and experiential" (Florida 2004, p. 33). It is precisely at this point that we can clearly see the importance of creative practices. Experimentation, knowledge and know-how exchange are not practices restricted to a single domain, but staples of creativity across every domain. They are, moreover, precisely the kind of methods, techniques and processes that result from the type of negotiation and collaboration enabled by a network. Flatter organizations that allow for more decentralized decision-making will more readily provide the right environment for these networks to flourish. They are more likely to attract workers who are expected to be part of interdisciplinary teams, have the skills or willingness to use a variety of technological tools and have the resilience to deal with outputs that cannot be fully anticipated.

At the actor level interdisciplinarity means that workers must, in a way, speak different languages, that is, be able to understand the knowledge and considerations of other actors, including non-human actors.[20] To name a case in point, within a creative agency, roles like communication strategist, copywriter, art director and producer entail very different types of knowledge and specific responsibilities. However, for a marketing

[19] At the individual level, Florida argues that workers within the Creative Class, whether artists, engineers, musicians, or computer scientists, share three important traits or values, "individuality, difference and merit" (Florida 2004, p. 8).

[20] Lazzarato (2010) expresses a similar idea when he describes creative work as work that is "more determined by 'action' than by 'production'. This does not signify the disappearance of handwork or physical labour, but the constitution of another assemblage in which manual labour and intellectual labour, 'material' labour and 'immaterial' labour, are caught up in a 'machinic' process, which can be found [...] in artistic institutions, the states, business, local collectives, criticism and the media" (p. 102).

campaign to be creative, they must all be able to not only understand each other, but also communicate their own views effectively, including a vision for the campaign that is not reduced to their specific perspective or to the use of only those technologies that they individually master. Success in doing so is by no means guaranteed, making the risk of failure a permanent fixture of creative networks. Unlike Adam Smith's famous pin factory, in an environment like this one, outputs cannot be fully predicted. Management may of course dictate the form of the output, say a TV commercial or a dozen social media posts, but they cannot predict the specific story that will be told, the type of values reflected in such a story, the tone, gravity or humour of the script, or the aesthetics of the film. Trying to exert full control over all aspects would mean disrupting the network's ability to function. This is no doubt often done in practice, but always at the cost of creativity—and many brands do choose control over creativity, which is why as consumers we are constantly bombarded by unimaginative, boring ads.

When business objectives, for instance, overrule the need to effectively understand and communicate with consumers, the result can easily be a message that is completely ignored by those same consumers, no matter how beautifully packaged it may be. If, however, an effective message is crafted along with a relevant and novel vehicle to deliver it, but producers fail to bring it to life, the result will still be a failed campaign. Interdisciplinarity is anything but easy and networks, as mentioned earlier, will always remain fragile structures. If a firm, whatever its size, lacks the resilience and commitment to learn from such failures and insists on fully controlling its creative networks, then it will simply be unable to benefit from the creativity advantages that Florida outlines.

Creativity challenges and changes the transactional nature of the relationships that exist within a corporate environment. It may, for this reason, seem ironic that it's Neoliberalism, arguably one of the most brutal versions of capitalism, that opened the door for creative networks. What it couldn't do is eliminate the constant tension between collaboration and subordination, between rule-following and negotiation, which is the bread and butter of any firm powered by members of the Creative Class. This tension arises when workers go from acting as intermediaries, to acting as powerful mediators. Technological development (the Internet, software, hardware, plug-ins, etc.) has played a decisive role in this respect too. Computer technologies have allowed workers to make experimentation and creativity profitable, and to do so without the need of constant managerial supervision. Despite the necessary autonomy and fragility of creative networks, they remain an attractive proposition for firms of all sizes, because creativity can add substantial value to existing products or services.

From a managerial perspective, the real difficulty comes from their inability to subordinate creative networks to the logic of meritocracy. In practice, meritocracy works by giving individual rewards based on individual performance. The problem, as has been shown, is that creativity is not the product of individuals, but of networks, and networks can only survive if they nurture collaboration and negotiation. Without collaboration old ideas can never be challenged. New ideas will seldom be trialled if benefits go to certain individuals within the network, while ignoring others. Neoliberalism's focus on individual rewards is simply ineffective in producing more and better creative outputs. As Dutch philosopher Henk Oosterling puts it, "creativity no longer resides in, but in-between individuals. Creativity is first and foremost relational. Cooperation, participation, and interaction no longer presuppose individuals. These come to the fore in creativity" (Oosterling 2007, p. 376).

Individuals, to be sure, play a role within a network. The individual remains an actor that proposes new ideas, new methods and new processes. The creative output will always be the result of a play of propositions among different actors within a network. Lev Manovich defines a creative output as the creation of something that is both novel and relevant (useful) for the spectator.[21] This remains true within the arts, true within advertising and true within any industry that wants to hire members of the Creative Class.

Neoliberalism's increased flexibility to hire and fire workers, while seemingly compatible with the need to maintain creative networks fresh, is a double-edged sword. Changing the actors within a network can, in principle, allow for new ideas and new practices to reinvigorate a network. Yet, the reality is that greater efficiency and cost reduction are the most common criteria behind hiring and firing decisions, not the continuous development of creativity. At the same time, the play and collaboration between workers and technologies means that every worker replaced may result in a significant loss of knowledge and know-how on collaboration. New actors within a network will always require new types of relationships to be

[21] Manovich (2023a) states: Indeed, many definitions of "creativity" agree on this point: "it is the creation of something that is both original and worthwhile or useful" (p. 6).

created and possible new roles defined. Mediators may need to become intermediaries and new black boxes may emerge as a response to changes made by managers, who are often weakly connected to the creative networks their decisions disturb. In practice, changes to creative teams will lead to changes to the type and quality of creative outputs. The reconstitution of the network will favour different priorities and can lead to entirely different orientations of the output created. Replacing, for instance, the creative director of an advertising team will mean, in practice, that outputs will also change in kind; a set of different aesthetics may be the most visible result, but it may also mean giving greater weight to certain type of creative output over other (e.g. cheeky copy over slick design, interactive physical experiences over emotionally charged TV commercials).

This is another reason why it's important to leave behind the idea of creativity being an individual's game. This doesn't deny the work of talented individuals. The point is that we live in a world where creativity requires a variety of talents to come together and collaborate in an effective manner. An important lesson from both Florida's ideas and my analysis of networks is that strict hierarchies do not lead to better creativity. Hierarchies stifle experimentation and, most importantly, hinder the challenging of old ideas, which is central for a network's outputs to remain novel and relevant.

Neoliberalism's powerful narrative about individual freedom and individual autonomy has been very effective in making the term "collective" feel anxiety inducing. Embracing the collective feels wrong, feels like we are giving up on our own sense of self. It feels like asking us to embrace a follower mentality. The power of Neoliberalism's brew of individualism is that it makes us forget that all such presumptions are purely ideological. It makes us forget that within a network an actor is only effective when it can collaborate and ally with others.[22]

Emptying the term collective from its Neoliberal baggage is a fundamental task of anyone who wants to become part of the Creative Class and of every firm that wants to benefit from creativity. Latour (2005) reminds us in this regard that the collective is not a fixed thing out there in the world that is exerting pressure over us, "but a movement of establishing

[22] Harman (2009) argues that within the ANT framework an actant's ability to affect reality can only be measured by the strength of its alliances: "Actors become more real by making large portions of the cosmos vibrate in harmony with their goals, or by taking detours in their goals to capitalise on the force of nearby actants" (p. 31).

provisional cohesion that will have to be started all over again every single day" (p. 147).

The network is a collective and a very fragile one. The network, however, doesn't constrain individuals, but amplifies them, giving them the ability to harness their own talents and bring them to life creatively. The lone individual moving others through sheer willpower is a fiction and an authoritarian fantasy, if we take its full consequences seriously. The enemy of the individual is not the collective, but status anxiety or what sociologist Richard Sennet (2012) calls invidious comparison. Corporate environments, he argues, often follow organizational models that discourage teamwork (from performance reviews to contract negotiations, everything is structured so as to make individuals feel inadequate and for the success of others to be seen as a detriment to their own success), while "competition for rewards hinders the sharing of information, decreases cooperation and makes people more risk averse" (Sennett 2008, p. 33). This reveals, perhaps surprisingly, that meritocracy's aim of fuelling individual productivity is, at its core, incompatible with higher creativity.

In previous chapters it's been argued that asking whether AI is creative cannot receive a proper answer within a paradigm of creativity that reduces it to an individual talent. Neoliberalism's emphasis on meritocracy and individual rewards runs counter to the need that creative networks have for negotiation, collaboration and the forging of strong alliances among actors. Focusing too much on the individual creator also bypasses the question of creative practice, which is needed to understand how a variety of networked actors work together to negotiate the vision of their output, and the expertise needed to achieve it. Such negotiations include those between the humans and the non-humans; we must keep in mind that within ANT objects and technologies are still actors. This may range from an actor's relationship to their working environment as well as to the variety of technologies that are seamlessly used across the Creative Class, from laptops and servers to cloud services and apps, all the way to today's AI systems. Actors' choices, such as to give stronger emphasis to design over story or video over photography, will impact any output reached. The better the actors within a network are at negotiating with others, the easier it will be for them to experiment, trial new ideas, challenge old ones and, ultimately, deliver higher creativity. The impact that AI systems will have on the Creative Class will depend, hence, on the type of role that such systems have and will have within the networks that power creativity, in the artworld and beyond.

AI Creativity: How Does It Work?

This book began with the question "Is AI creative?". The analysis of creativity within as well as outside the artworld has shown that the right question to ask about AI creativity is not "what it is" but "how does it work". Asking what it is would mean remaining within a paradigm that sees creativity as a capability that would somehow be present or active inside an AI system. In more formal terms, "[a]sking 'what it is' is to frame the work within a metaphysics of truth, of essence and representation, but 'what is it for me' poses a question concerning the forces involved within the thing and a question of subjectivity" (Zepke 2014, p. 17).

If creativity is networked, then thinking about how AI works amounts to asking about the role that it plays or can play within current and future creative networks. The ideal scenario would be one where an AI system takes the role of a unique mediator within creative networks. A mediator that supports the flow of new ideas, the challenging of old ones and the generation of relevant novelty. It is also a question about the effective space for negotiation between humans and AI systems, whether it creates space for collaboration between humans and AI to explore new perspectives which humans alone cannot.

The undesirable scenario would on the contrary be one in which AI systems disrupt creative networks, hindering their ability to deliver relevant novelty.[23] The risk under that scenario is to fall into predictable and unoriginal results, results that, for example, favour outputs created by AI systems alone, create barriers between human and AI system interaction or favour control over collaboration by predetermining the creative space of any potential output. It is when thinking of this second scenario that AI systems, Gen AI in particular, are meant to replace or automate creativity. This is not a story about robots replacing human bodies at their jobs, but as researchers Bueno et al. (2023) point out, "Generative AI is a way of tightening control over the creative aspect of labour power without sacrificing the required flexibility and novelty required by the creative industries, while also maintaining the tendency towards precarity in contractual relations that have defined these industries" (p. 8).

[23] Digital Art researcher Stella Sofokleous (2022) takes this argument further, noting that the debate over the potentially autonomous artistic production of a non-human agent is a complicated one, partly because it brings back the modernistic concern that the machine will displace the artist from the creative process leading to a dystopian technological totalitarianism.

Do AI systems replace human actors or collaborate with them? What type of actor is ChatGPT or DALL-E? Framing this question within a narrative of automation or replacement means asking whether AI systems can imitate the output produced by today's creative networks, so as to render the latter obsolete.

On the question of imitation, writer, researcher and artist Joanna Zylinska (2020) argues that a focus on outputs is often accompanied with a reduction of creativity to the ability to replicate the structures and patterns that are found in music, painting or literature, referred to often as style.[24] Imitation, she continues, leads even the most thoughtful engagement with AI creativity to define it as a machine's ability to copy such styles (Zylinska, p. 49). While somewhat similar to the notion of mastery of technique explored earlier, the recognition of patterns and structure occurs at a higher level of abstraction that cannot be reduced to, for example, the muscle memory that we find in a piano virtuoso or a heart surgeon. Focusing on style predetermines the type of creative output that is deemed suitable or appropriate. In other words, the style in question serves as a frame of reference against which all creative outputs are judged.

Art curators are well known for their recognition of style, and their expertise lies often in their uncanny ability to separate the cheap imitators from the valuable original. This is true about the style of individual artists, but it's equally true when referring to artistic movements such as expressionism, which finds an outlet through a variety of mediums, including the visual arts, architecture and music. The recognition of style is by no means creative in itself but has important implications on how the general public understands creativity and whether it values something due to that same creativity. The best way to understand these implications comes through the idea of the Turing Test. The idea of the traditional Turing Test is simple: a human interacts through a screen or through remote means with another form of intelligence and through that interaction must judge whether the other intelligence in question is human or artificial. If the human is unable to distinguish whether they are talking to a human or an artificial intelligence and they are in fact interacting with an AI, then the system in question has passed the Turing Test and can be labelled as intelligent. The traditional test can be translated into a creativity Turing Test,

[24] Zylinska argues, "This mechanism is revealed most explicitly in the public and, inevitably, curatorial fascination with what we may call 'ai imitation work', also known as 'style transfer' " (p. 50).

which would develop as follows: a human is presented with a creative output and must in turn determine whether such output was created by a human intelligence or by an artificial one. If the human is unable to distinguish between both, then the AI in question has passed the Turing Test and can be labelled as creative.

Following my analysis it should be clear by now that a creativity Turing Test is not useful as a way of determining whether an AI is creative, but it is certainly a measure of whether a specific type of output will be judged as creative by other humans. It is in this narrower sense that the test can have an impact on creativity; on the way we view and understand creativity. Most humans judge creativity based on the object they see, without spending too much time thinking about the process behind its creation, making the impact of the Turing Test easy to see. Much of the debate around the relevance of this type of Turing Test focused on what Alan Turing himself called the Lovelace objection, that is, on the idea that creativity remains a uniquely human feature and "machines can, at most, merely imitate the appearance of creativity" (Bueno et al. 2023, p. 1). This objection relates to the persistent humanism analysed in Chap. 1 of this book and its ideological prerogative to define creativity as an exclusively human trait. From this perspective passing the creativity Turing Test becomes a threat to its deep-held beliefs about human nature.[25] For this reason, it's still relevant to take a closer look into the implications of the Turing Test's ability to define how the term creativity is understood and used in our daily lives. Arielli and Manovich (2022) remind us of the importance of the context of the test itself: "we need to ask ourselves under which condition—if any—we would use notions like "thinking" (or "intelligence" and "creativity") to describe non-human, artificial entities" (p. 5).

If the context is such that creativity is seen mainly, or entirely, as the ability to reproduce a style, as is the case of the GAN models discussed in Chap. 1, then the implication is that creative networks are not needed for creativity to exist. From this vantage point the Turing Test "would instead show to what extent humans can be mechanical in their processes and behaviours" (Arielli and Manovich, p. 10). This conclusion by Arielli and Manovich ultimately brings the discussion of mastery of a technique back

[25] Sofokleous (2022) sums up the issue stating that "The main problem in the future acceptance of a creative system as an artist per se lies in the fact that throughout the spectrum of historical narratives of art, the creative process has been identified with human nature itself" (p. 558).

into the conversation. However, the way in which such mastery is judged is based on its output alone. It's irrelevant whether an AI system learns the way humans learn, whether it expresses intent or it doesn't. What matters is whether the AI system can deliver outputs that can rightfully belong to a recognized style. A style that has been recognized as an expression or embodiment of creativity. Such recognition, as stated earlier, doesn't happen in a vacuum, but is determined by the historical context in which a creative output is generated.

It is only when moving away from imitation that the question of whether AI is creative becomes meaningful again. AI and media scholar Matteo Pasquinelli and Joler (2021) points to the particular elements that we must take into account if we want to move further:

> The hackneyed question 'Can AI be creative?' should be reformulated in technical terms: is machine learning able to create works that are not imitations of the past? Is machine learning able to extrapolate beyond the stylistic boundaries of its training data? The 'creativity' of machine learning is limited to the detection of styles from the training data and then random improvisation within these styles. (p. 1275)

Why can't the current AI system (LLMs) be able to learn beyond style? Why can't they improvise? The answer is technical in nature but has to do with the way in which such systems learn. A pre-training phase is necessary for AI systems to be able to respond to a prompt or query. Whether its responses are purely text-based, like ChatGPT, or goes from text-to-image like Midjourney, the principle of pre-training remains the same. A neural network learns using existing data. Its process of learning is statistical in nature. The model learns or rather teaches itself to recognize patterns between texts, in the case of ChatGPT or between classified images, in the case of Midjourney. Classification is not the end goal of any such AI system, but rather the first step of the pre-training phase. The real feat of an AI system is its ability to discover patterns between seemingly disconnected images and their context. These patterns are multidimensional in nature, making it almost impossible for a human to be able to understand, in many cases, the type of connections that an AI system can make between images or texts. Like any statistical model using aggregate data, it will be biased towards certain associations, based on the frequency in which such associations can be found within its training data. Take, for example, a prompt asking an AI system to create a photographic depiction of a neurosurgeon. If during the pre-training phase the machine learned that most depictions of neurosurgeons are middle-aged, white, men, then it's likely to return as a response to the prompt, a neurosurgeon that is a white middle-aged man. No AI system is able to actually survey, sticking to the example, the universe of neurosurgeons to be able to know whether the depictions in the data are in fact proper representations of that universe. The system cannot judge either, whether gender, age, ethnicity or any other marker is relevant to being a neurosurgeon. In fact, the system is not able to distinguish between an actual image of a doctor at work and an image of an actor playing a doctor in a TV show. This overall learning process and response to queries based on statistics means that an LLM is fundamentally constrained to the data that is used in its training, as well as to the distribution of objects, contexts, people within that data.[26] This is precisely why Pasquinelli is not surprised that AI systems are pretty good at recognizing styles. It's also why he claims that for AI to be creative we must analyse whether it's autonomous, whether it can understand novel cases and generate novel responses, and whether it can effectively collaborate with a creative network.

While all three aspects are connected, it now makes sense to dive deeper into the issue of autonomy. The issue of autonomy is not entirely disconnected from the discussion of the creativity Turing Test. AI researcher Caterina Moruzzi (2022) states that people who have participated in a Turing Test "overwhelmingly agree on qualifying AI as a tool, animated at least in part, by their fear of "giving up control to machines in the process of creation" and "this opposition toward the attribution of creativity to artificial systems was grounded on a resolute belief that AI cannot, and should not, be creative since it lacks the necessary personality, feelings, and emotions that are prerequisite for creative agency"" (p. 15). The concept

[26] Zylinska (2020) is harsher in her description of current AI systems stating that "Much of what passes off for AI today is really a product of coupling big data with statistical analysis. impressive or even mysterious as some of the outcomes may look, they are the result of advanced calculations performed on large quantities of data. New AI is therefore first and foremost a sophisticated agent of pattern recognition: a post-cyberpunk incarnation of William Gibson's character from his eponymous 2003 novel in which advertising consultant Cayce Pollard had an almost superhuman ability to make connections and find meanings within the flow of marketing data" (P 25).

Zylinska, J. (2020). AI art: machine visions and warped dreams. Open humanities press. P 25.

of autonomy, just like creativity and intelligence, is one that can be often trapped within the humanist paradigm.

Looking into the ways in which Computer Science and AI researchers define agency can be a useful first step away from the paradigm. Moruzzi follows Russel and Norvig (2011) in this regard. They argued that an important difference often emerges when comparing agency as defined in Computer Science against its definition by AI researchers. In Computer Science the emphasis is on autonomy, understood as the agent's ability to adapt and learn from an environment, while in AI research agency is mostly seen as "anything that can be viewed as perceiving its environment through sensors and acting upon that environment through actuators" (Moruzzi 2022, p. 3). The emphasis of AI on autonomous physical movement and response is simply irrelevant when discussing current AI systems, in particular Gen AI. Only if we take their training as a form of environment can we say that current AI systems have the ability to adapt and learn from an environment. What Moruzzi shows is that from the perspective of Computer Science we may reasonably say that AI systems are autonomous, yet the same thing cannot be said from the perspective of AI research. This means that we must find recourse in a different notion of autonomy, which is another advantage that can be found in Latour's ANT framework.

It's been argued that an actor's agency within the ANT framework is entirely determined by the role it plays within a network. Its ability to influence other actors depends, in turn, by its ability to effectively mobilize their talents, skills and experience. What this tells us is that an actor's autonomy is not defined by its ability to disconnect itself from a network, but on the contrary, that stronger connections are a sign of greater autonomy. Autonomy, therefore, must be judged based on an actor's ability to influence others or be influenced by them. If an actor cannot have agency outside of a network, this implies that autonomy is not judged based on how well an agent or actor frees itself from society. Instead, connection among actors is central to the way societies function, attesting to the social nature of agency in ANT, in line as well with systems theory.[27]

Stating that AI systems are autonomous, or that they lack autonomy, within a particular theoretical framework may still seem abstract and its

[27] Moruzzi (2022) highlights that Systems Theory "calls attention to the social nature of agency, emphasising how communication between agents is a central feature of society and social processes" (p. 3).

consequences hard to follow. However, the core issue of autonomy can be phrased through a simple statement: if AI systems are tools, then they cannot be autonomous. Few would argue that AI systems are a tool in the sense that a hammer or a can opener is a tool. Despite this, as McLoughlin (2024) points out, we have traditionally defined computer technology as a set of tools: "the computer was no more than a tool. It is as unrealistic (to suggest that the programmer was not the author) as it would be to suggest that, if you write your work with a pen, it is the pen which is the author of the work rather than the person who drives the pen" (p. 5).

Seeing AI systems as tools is more than simply claiming that they are useful for a task. It's more than a description of an object's utility. As discussed, when analysing computational creativity, defining computer technologies as mere tools is challenging, because the way in which a creator relates to them may often escape the master-servant relationship that implies that a tool's actions are nothing but an extension of its master's will. When we say something is a tool, say a hammer, we presuppose a clear hierarchy (the hammer does what its wielder wants and nothing else) and a range of action (the hammer can hit a nail, but it cannot tell you the time). The perfect tool, hence, offers no resistance, only compliance; it does as it's told. Whatever the tool can and will do depends exclusively on who wields it or commands it. When we say that humans are not a means to an end, we literally mean that they are not tools. We say humans are not tools because we believe they have a certain degree of autonomy that cannot be taken away from them. Freedom to move, to express an opinion, among other political freedoms, is the direct result of our core belief that humans are not tools.

Are AI Systems Autonomous?

The master-servant relationship characterizes the way humans relate to their tools. By the same token, whether we are talking about computers or hammers, the reality is that there is no perfect tool, because every tool will offer some resistance. We experience this resistance every time a hammer breaks, because it was used too forcefully or every time, we have to deal with a printer leaving unexplainable ink lines on a document. Tools and machines break down, malfunction and age, making them less malleable and more difficult to command. Resistance is, however, more than just a break or disruption that should be avoided. Creators, for example, can purposefully engage with this resistance, as Jackson Pollock did with his dripping techniques. Resistance overall is the norm rather than the exception with our tools, including the algorithms that power our software.[28] The master-servant relationship is, hence, never perfect, because control is never total. This makes autonomy a relative rather than an absolute term. As stated earlier an autonomous actor is not one that has successfully detached itself from a historical context. We can compare, in turn, the relative autonomy of one actor to another. When claiming that a creator is autonomous, this meant that they are able to respond to that historical context in novel ways. The dynamics of deterritorialization and territorialization found in the work of contemporary artists do exactly this: respond to a state of affairs by challenging its prejudices and offering novel ways to rethink the role of things and concepts within a particular domain, as well as within our daily lives. This is precisely why Deleuze and Guattari (1994) claim that "[t]here is no other aesthetic problem than that of the insertion of art into everyday life" (p. 293).

In a similar manner, asking whether AI systems are autonomous must be seen as a relative not an absolute question. What degree of autonomy do they have in comparison to other technologies and can that significantly change in the near future?

Sofokleous (2022) notices that at first glance the autonomy of AI systems would be "mitigated due to the need to interact with the human agent, who in part determines the operation of the system through programming" (p. 557). From this perspective AI systems would be seen as having the same autonomy as any other piece of software, given that human interaction is essential for it to deliver an output. Yet, she continues, this assertion misses the fact that machine learning, understood as a particular set of algorithms, remains an autonomous entity inasmuch as it "operates independently of its inputs" (p. 557). Therefore, we cannot judge the autonomy of an AI system based solely on whether it can operate without human input, but we should also take into account whether it can "exist independently of the data on which it operates or the program that encodes it" (p. 557).

[28] Johanna Drucker (2013), referring to a more general description of the executive nature of algorithmic behaviour, notes: "Algorithms are instructions for processes, for performances, whose outcomes may usually be predictable, but of course, are as open to error and random uncertainties in their execution as they are to uncertain outcomes in their use at the higher level of their operation and use" (p. 3).

Along these lines, researcher Rob Kitchin (2017) points out, the algorithm is inherently performative in the sense that it can contribute to the implementation of many alternative scenarios: "algorithms are rarely fixed in form and their work in practice unfolds in multifarious ways. As such, algorithms need to be recognised as being ontogenetic, performative and contingent: that is, they are never fixed in nature, but are emergent and constantly unfolding" (p. 21).

Unlike traditional rule-based algorithms, GAN (Generative Adversarial Network) algorithms don't work by setting domain-specific rules that fix a relationship among different variables. Instead, as explained by Amoore (2023), "deep learning is understood to decompose a problem into multiple layers of representation of patterns in the data (often called 'hidden layers'). In this specific sense, deep learning algorithms are more experimental and open-ended in their computation than past rules-based forms" (p. 24).[29] Deep learning algorithms are, therefore, not merely a more advanced version of previous rules-based algorithms, but are better seen as Computer Science's response to a world where issues are multidimensional, where there is a greater bounty of data (so-called Big Data) and where rule-based approaches have proven to be limited or unfit. This is why prompting a Gen AI cannot be reduced to a set of axioms or principles. It's also why responses to similar or identical prompts may deliver different results; the more data is fed into the machine and the more it learns from previous prompts, the more it's likely to adapt its future responses.

One of the best ways to understand this relative autonomy of Gen AI over other recent technologies is through the work of artist and researcher

[29] Deep learning is a unique approach to machine learning. Where past approaches to machine learning began with the engineering of domain-specific rules that captured the relationship of variables within a dataset, deep learning decomposes a problem into multiple layers of representation of patterns in the data. In this specific sense, deep learning algorithms are more experimental and open-ended in their computation than past rules-based forms. Computer scientist and godfather of AI Geoff Hinton describes the difference between rules and learned features as follows: some problems cannot be addressed using rules, making programming difficult. Instead of writing a program manually for each specific task, the machine learning approach gathers lots of instances, clusters them and provides a representation of the data in terms of features it has "learned" (Amoore 2023). Here one begins to see the implications arise: there are problems so complex, entailing multiple dimensions, that it is no longer possible for a human engineer to determine the relevant variables that define the rules that would allow them to write the program, choosing instead for a deep learning approach.

Jon McCormack. In his 2023 installation *The World We Made*, McCormack explores the AI-generated images critically assessing the way in which these AI systems depict our human world and in doing so shape, in turn, our own understanding of that same world. His installation depicts a large number of images generated by Midjourney to depict living persons. He uses single-term prompts including, "woman", "grandmother", "mother with baby" and "middle aged man", among others. We know that the images depicted will be based entirely on its training data and thus are likely to show the most common depictions based on that data. He notes that at a first glance AI-generated images display a faux sense of high production value and editorial style yet the people depicted are, to be sure, not real people. This becomes obvious as we look closer and realize that the images are full of imperfections and oddities that question AI's ability to produce coherence. Especially striking is the fact that the figures depicted appear to be lost in a gallery of mirrors and are often trying to photograph themselves using a smartphone. There was nothing in the prompts that required such a setting; no prompt asking for a smartphone to be included. The output to these simple prompts shows, on the one hand, that the system has made decisions that are entirely disconnected from the prompt itself. On the other hand, the images, while unique, depict a strangely generic aspect to them that makes them feel stale and repetitive (Fig. 2.2).

Can AI Systems Generate Novelty?

The previous section argued that an actor's autonomy is a relative, not an absolute term, when it comes to defining their ability to impact creative outputs. The text has shown how the question of AI autonomy can be linked to the type of decisions that AI systems make when depicting people, for example, based on human prompts. While McCormack's example was specific to Midjourney, other Gen AI systems make similar decisions, no matter if they generate texts, video or any other potential output. The statistical nature of all LLMs means that these conclusions can be safely extended to systems like ChatGPT and DALL-E, among others.

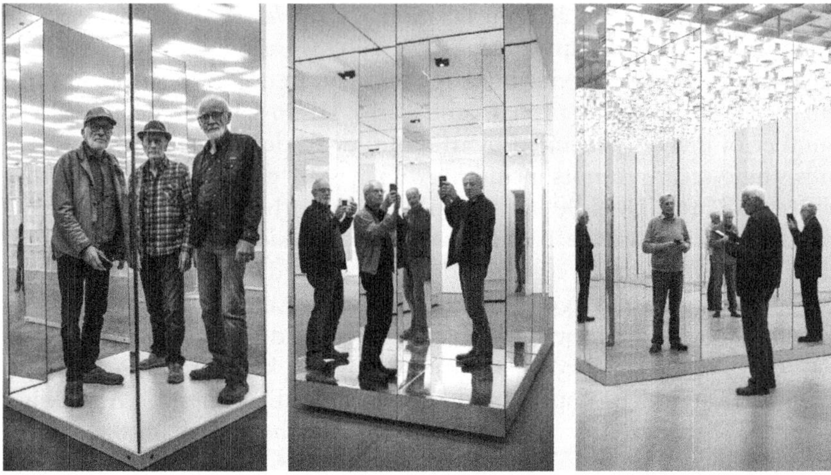

Fig. 2.2 Three prompted AI-generated images as part of Jon McCormack (2023) *The World We Made*. Credits to Jon McCormack (Fair Use for educational purpose)

The issue of AI's ability to generate novelty is, however, another matter altogether.[30] As already hinted in the study of McCormack's work Gen AI is seriously limited in its ability to generate novelty. This is not accidental, but again the result of the way in which LLMs work.[31] The statistical nature of deep learning algorithms gives enormous weight to the most common, to the average over anything else. The inability of human prompts to challenge this limitation raises the risk of turning AI systems into black boxes, which is a role that recognizes their autonomy, but

[30] From a philosophical perspective Fazi (2019) claims the problem is still related to the humanist bias on agency, outlined earlier in this text. In her words "the popular belief about the impossibility of novelty in computation could be said to be a consequence, or at least to reflect, the fundamental ontological disparity between machines on the one hand, and the non-mechanical on the other" (p. 819).

[31] Pasquinelli and Joler (2021) shows this is an issue that goes beyond Gen AI: "A logical limit of machine learning classification, or pattern recognition, is the inability to recognise a unique anomaly that appears for the first time, such as a new metaphor in poetry, a new joke in everyday conversation, or an unusual obstacle (a pedestrian? a plastic bag?) on the road. The undetection of the new (something that has never 'been seen' by a model and therefore never classified before in a known category) is a particularly hazardous problem for self-driving cars and one that has already caused fatalities" (p. 1275).

cannot explain it. If this is the case, then the ability for human-AI collaboration may be jeopardized. McCormack et al. (2023) present an example that help us understand the limitations of current AI systems, when it comes to novelty. The authors use two prompts to illustrate the issue: the first prompt is "an astronaut riding a horse" and the second "a horse riding an astronaut" (p. 6). As seen in figure 9.2 the system returned two images, both depicting an astronaut riding a horse, despite the second prompt having an entirely different meaning. The reason for these two images being basically the same depiction has everything to do with the type of statistical associations that AI systems establish. None of the current AI systems analyses a sentence semantically. This means, continuing with the example, that they aren't aware about why riding a horse means something different from riding an astronaut. All they do is provide a response, in this case an image response, based on the most probable associations found in their datasets (Fig. 2.3).

Novelty, however, doesn't necessarily require an AI system to have a better grasp about the meaning of a prompt in order to return a novel response. Artist Leonel Moura's (2018) *Artists and Robots* show at the

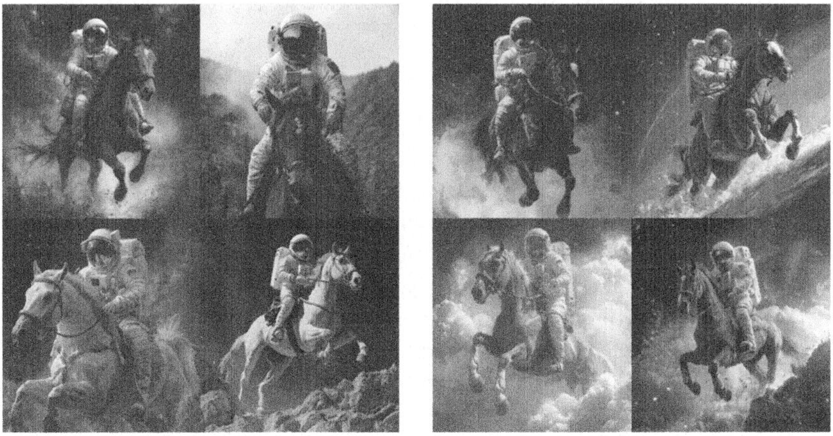

Fig. 2.3 Midjourney-generated images that replicate McCormack's experiment, albeit with a 2024 version of the system. To the right, a set of images based on the text prompt: "an astronaut riding a horse" and to the left a set of images based on the text prompt: "a horse riding an astronaut". Both sets of images are almost identical in nature, despite the very different prompts used

Grand Palais in Paris illustrates this point well. The art show proposes collaboration as a form of pedagogical discovery that delivers unexpected results. The work is precisely intended to address the issue of whether a machine can be creative or whether they should be seen as mere tools (Moura 2018, p. 1). At the centre of the work are Moura's *artbots*, which are relatively simple machines that can move across a surface, armed with a microchip and sensors to detect obstacles and a colour pen to draw lines as they move around (Moura, pp. 1–2). They move randomly inside an initially white arena, detecting the colour beneath them. Depending on how much colour each robot senses, it either raises or lowers its pen once a specific threshold is met. From a random start, the process develops in a unique manner, generating unique patterns and colours. Inspired by ants, Moura wants to show how its bots can jointly work together to generate novel artwork, albeit without any predefined direction or any awareness about their role within the creative process (Moura, pp. 2–3). In his words:

> [R]obots like those I use are able to generate novelty, it must also be recognized that they have at least some degree of creativity ... the emergent process implies that the resulting artworks cannot be predetermined by the person who initiates the process ... The algorithm and the basic rules introduced thereby via the robot microchip are not so very different, furthermore, from education. (Moura, p. 3)

Moura's artbots can be categorized as an exercise that is intended to deliver unexpected results through the introduction of a comparable randomness to the one seen in Pollock. The robots are not based on LLMs, nor can they be classified more broadly as AI systems. These are simply robots whose programming allows for (seemingly) unpredictable results to emerge. Learning here is truly a metaphor and not related to the term machine learning. Moura's artbots also show that creators can collaborate with "dumb technologies" to produce novelty. Collaboration, as this case shows, does not presuppose an equality of intelligence, nor does it presuppose that all agencies involved do so on equal footing. Collaboration, as the artbots show, results from Moura's ability to test and play with the bot's resistance. Greater autonomy means greater resistance, and it means that Moura needs to adapt as well: changing the size of the arena, the number of artbots that fit in it, the range of motion of each bot and the starting point. Moura realized that for the results of the artbots to be novel, he had to give them greater autonomy, which in turn meant that he had to give up control over their actions. Furthermore, for the collaboration to work, Moura had to first and foremost avoid confining his relationship with the artbots to the master-servant paradigm. He does so, to restate, by giving up control over a variety of key elements, from the movement of the bots to the type of patterns that can emerge. For Moura, neither his artbots nor AI take over the creative process, but rather pave the way for a symbiotic dialogue between humans and machines, in an effort to achieve common artistic goals.[32]

His relationship to the artbots cannot be reduced to his control over them, but to the balance he achieves by negotiating with the bots, in order to achieve results that he could not achieve on his own or predict on beforehand. In a way we can say that the artbots multiply his creativity, by unlocking creative outputs that were not available to him alone. His proposal, to conclude, can be seen as rephrasing the question "can AI be creative?" to "can AI augment human creativity?".

Augmented Creativity: AI as a Multiplier of Creativity

Simply put, augmented creativity can be summed up as follows: "Humans and machines have different strengths, and instead of trying to squeeze machines into a way of thinking that is human, we should aim to develop computer systems that make the most of their power" (Pease and Colton 2011, p. 4). By rethinking Moura's artbots through this lens, we can define their role within a creative network as a particular type of mediator. While we can't claim that they are collaborators in the same way as another human actor can be a collaborator, we cannot reduce them to mere tools either. Instead, the idea of augmented creativity invites us to think of the artbots and of AI tools more broadly, as actors that allow humans to interact with the world in non-human ways, as well as actors that can show us what it is to see the world with non-human eyes.

Moura's artbots are a perfect example of a machine that allows us to explore new ways of interacting with the world. Their sensors are by no means an imitation of our human senses, but entirely different ways to explore and engage with the world around us. They are not meant to imitate or replicate how a human would respond to a given situation. Their

[32] He adds on his online manifesto, "Humans are no longer concerned about the direct production of objects but dedicate all their knowledge and energy to create and cooperate with an imaginary, non-human life that is devoted to art-making" (Moura 2004).

role is to help us imagine how a different interaction with the world can lead to unexpectedly creative outputs. In the case of Gen AI, it's best to see them as an example of seeing the world with non-human eyes. We know LLMs specifically are able to process billions of parameters of data, beyond the capacity of any human. Using this data, they can create multi-dimensional maps of the relationships that exist between objects in our texts, images, videos, etc., which is again something that goes beyond our human abilities. These associations or relationships may often feel odd, arbitrary and completely absurd as in, for example, the tendency of such systems to portray certain professionals as white men. However, such shortcomings are actually a reflection of ourselves. They show us the many arbitrary and often absurd relationships that our own understanding of the world entails. They reveal uneven relationships of power based on geographies, culture and class, among others. This revelatory aspect of our own worldview can function as a means for deterritorialization and may allow creators to think about contexts, problems and concepts in novel ways.[33]

The term augmented creativity, however, precedes the dawn of our current AI systems and can be traced back to pioneer in the study of human-computer interaction Douglas Engelbart, who in 1962 wrote a paper titled *Augmenting the Human Intellect: A Conceptual Framework*. In it, Engelbart (2023) discusses the *memex*, an idea coming from Vannevar Bush, who headed the US Office of Scientific Research and Development during World War II. Vannevar Bush imagines the memex as a "device in which an individual stores all his books, records, and communications, and which is mechanized so that it may be consulted with exceeding speed and flexibility. It is an enlarged intimate supplement to his memory" (Bush 1945, p. 101). Were we standing in the early 1990s we wouldn't be at fault for seeing Bush's memex as a close description of a personal computer. From our vantage point, Pieters and Winiger (2016) rightly point out that,

> "while entirely mechanical, Bush describes a device that features hyperlinked text, aggregated notes and bookmarks all extending human capacity to research and process information: The web"[34]. More importantly, what

[33] Sofokleous (2022) states a similar point when arguing that "[d]ue to the possibility of autonomous function of such systems, a large number of artists and programmers approach their relationship with their machines as a collaboration, a kind of an assemblage of living and non-living entities to achieve common artistic goals" (p. 555).

[34] Roelof Pieters & Samim Winiger. Accessed on Dec. 5, 2024. https://medium.com/@creativeai/creativeai-9d4b2346faf3#b28b

> Engelbart saw in Bush's memex, was the creative potential of a machine that would allow us to gather and integrate disparate information more easily, serving as an extension of our own minds. Engelbart's vision didn't focus on our ability to automate processes alone, but perhaps more importantly, emphasised how computer technologies can "multiply the power of people and collaborators by creating systems that augment our intellect, humanity and creativity" and ultimately "raise the human potential".

Using computers, and especially AI, to augment our creativity is, in any case, anything but a given. Like most types of collaboration, it cannot be taken for granted. It's not easy and can often lead to a use of computers that seems to follow this collaborative spirit, yet fails to impress, upon a closer look. Arielli and Manovich refer to this use of AI systems as a contemporary form of *Mannerism*, which was a highly criticized movement, blamed for reducing art to style, technique and imitation.[35] They provide two specific examples to illustrate the point: an AI system tasked with finishing Schubert's "Unfinished Symphony" (n. 8, 1822) in 2019 and another system tasked with completing Beethoven's unfinished 10th symphony as part of the celebration of the 250th anniversary of his birth (Arielli and Manovich 2022, p. 3). The first example turned out to be the result of a composer cherry-picking the best melodies the system generated and in the second example the system was fed specific variants of preexisting styles to ensure the relevance of the output (Arielli and Manovich, p. 3). These examples show that an AI system cannot generate completely new songs or styles, but instead, remain within a specific stylistic space, making it a form of computational *mannerism*.

Both examples show how easy it is to introduce computers in a creative process, when their role is to be an appendage to the work done by humans. From the perspective of the public, it's easy to be fooled by such examples, for the creative process that leads to the output may be fully concealed or even rhetorically dressed as something it is not. The failure in these two examples boils down to their lack of novelty, which in line with Manovich is an essential feature of creativity. In both cases the collaboration between humans and AI systems seemed to be more driven by the novelty of using an AI, rather than by a real interest in achieving something that a collaboration among humans alone cannot. Augmented

[35]The rich history and perspectives on Mannerism go beyond the scope of this book. For an in-depth study of the topic see Van den Akker, P. (2010). Looking for Lines: Theories of the Essence of Art and the Problem of Mannerism. Amsterdam University Press.

creativity is not merely a description of the way creators use AI systems. It's better seen as an invitation for creators to rethink their relationship to technology, including today's most advanced AI systems. It works only when the creator overcomes the urge to reduce AI to a tool, allowing them to see the, at times difficult to grasp, capabilities of these complex machines as opportunities for experimentation. Beyond our present, augmented creativity can also shape the way in which the Creative Class at large relates to future systems, which will be trained on even larger volumes of data and will likely have greater ability to generate associations and more complex multidimensional maps. Future systems may offer more advanced capabilities too, in terms of communicating with their human counterparts and making experimentation feel more like a joint effort rather than mainly human led. Chapter 3 will explore the type of collaborative model that would allow creators to augment their creativity as well as the barriers that such type of collaboration will meet in the face of economic forces that will continue to see higher productivity as the sole measure of success.

Before moving further, however, it's important to recap some of the key elements explored so far. Chapter 2 of this book has argued that the role of creativity in today's world is not confined to the artworld, but finds a place across a variety of industries, making it an aspiration for millions of creators worldwide. The study of Csikszentmihalyi's systems theory of creativity showed that to understand creativity we needed to step aside from the idea of creators being isolated individuals. Instead, he argued, creativity entails a continuous flow of ideas between personal background, culture and society. This view pushed us to rethink creativity as an essentially social phenomenon. Furthermore, such a view is compatible with Latour's ANT and, more generally, helped explain why novelty is not the result of a creator escaping their historical context, but rather responding to it, in a relevant way.

The text has argued that economic changes, driven by the establishment of Neoliberalism as the dominant ideology, were fundamental in opening the door to creative networks across a variety of industries. Following Florida's ideas on the Creative Class helps one trace the growth of these networks based on the realization that creativity adds value to a firm's goods and services. Over 20 years have passed since Florida's ideas on the Creative Class hit the shelves, yet creativity remains a fundamental component of today's economy. According to the Economist Intelligence Unit (2021), the Creative Sector employs more young people (aged

15–29) than any other sector. The advertising industry, for instance, has in the past decade seen its revenue skyrocket across the globe: the industry has seen 175% growth in the US, 156% in Western Europe, 159% in the Asia Pacific region, 199% in Latin America and over 156% in Africa during that time span (Statista 2024b). The video game industry is yet another example of the increased relevance of the Creative Class in today's economy, with a staggering 166% revenue growth in the past five years and an expected 145% revenue growth in the coming five (Statista 2024a). Another interesting example is the growth of content creators, which inhabit all major social platforms today. According to YouTube's parent company, Alphabet, YouTube creators alone upload 30,000 hours of new video content per hour (Statista 2022). All such figures show that the dawn of revolutionary technologies over the past three decades (e.g. the Internet, the personal computer and the smartphone) have not diminished the creative appetite of today's generation of workers. If anything, technology has played a key role in the development of flatter and more decentralized organizations: technologies allowed remotely located employees to collaborate; they allowed for more information to be gathered and used and made innovative ways to test and experiment more feasible.

More porous firms allowed new ideas, new skills and new ways of working to become the norm in sectors such as advertising, design, film, music and architecture among others. Yet, while Neoliberalism may have created an opportunity for the Creative Class, it's equally true that a strong tension between efficiency and creativity persists and is arguably the main risk that all creative networks face to this day. The future of the Creative Class is by no means certain and AI systems play an ambivalent role in this respect. While AI systems can potentially be used to create new avenues for exploration, as the concept of augmented creativity suggests, they can also be used to increase control over workers and often displace them, as Acemoglu and Johnson emphasized, using Amazon warehouses as an example of egregious control.

Yet, the narrative that emphasizes productivity and economic growth is fundamental to the adoption of current AI systems. It's equally fundamental in guiding the conversation towards the economic benefits of AI, while closing any meaningful talk about the risks to the least powerful players in that same economic system: employees, freelancers and small companies. It would be naive to expect this persuasive economic narrative centred around productivity to simply go away. The reality is that it's likely to continue shaping not only the adoption, but also the future development of AI systems. The last part of this book will look towards the future. It will study the tendencies that will shape the development of AI systems in the coming decade and their impact on creativity.

References

Acemoglu, D., and S. Johnson. 2023. *Power and progress: Our thousand-year struggle over technology and prosperity*. Hachette.

Amoore, L. 2023. Machine learning political orders. *Review of International Studies* 49 (1): 20–36.

Andrews, E., and P. Croal. 2023. ONS average household income, UK: 1977–2022. *Office for National Statistics*, January 25. https://www.ons.gov.uk/peoplepopulationandcommunity/personalandhouseholdfinances/incomeandwealth/bulletins/householddisposableincomeandinequality/financialyearending2022.

Arielli, E., and L. Manovich. 2022. AI-aesthetics and the anthropocentric myth of creativity. *Philpapers.org*: 1–16.

Baar, A. 2024. Forrester: 91% of US ad agencies are currently using, exploring Generative AI. *Marketing Dive*, June 24. https://www.marketingdive.com/news/forrester-Generative-ai-marketing-agencies-report/719285/. Accessed 25 Feb 2025.

Becker, G. 1978. *The mad genius controversy*. Sage Publications, Inc.

Boltanski, L., and E. Chiapello. 2002. The new spirit of capitalism [conference session]. *Conference of Europeanists*, March 14–16, 1–29. Chicago.

Brewer, P.R., et al. 2024. Artists or art thieves? Media use, media messages, and public opinion about artificial intelligence image generators. *AI & Society*: 77–87.

Bueno, C.C., P.S. Chow, and A. Popowicz. 2023. Not 'what', but 'where is creativity?': Towards a relational-materialist approach to Generative AI. *AI & Society*: 1–13.

Bush, V. 1945. As we may think. *Atlantic Monthly*, July: 101–108.

Caporal, J. 2024. How many Americans own stock? About 162 million – But the wealthiest 1% own more than half. *The Motley Fool*, September 23. https://www.fool.com/research/how-many-americans-own-stock/.

Chui, M., et al. 2024. The economic potential of generative AI: The next productivity frontier. *McKinsey & Company Report*, June 14. https://www.mckinsey.com/capabilities/mckinsey-digital/our-insights/The-economic-potential-of-Generative-AI-The-next-productivity-frontier#introduction. Accessed 25 Feb 2025.

Csikszentmihalyi, M. 2014. Society, culture, and person: A systems view of creativity. In *The systems model of creativity and its applications*, 47–61. Springer.

Deck, A. 2022. *AI-generated art sparks furious backlash from Japan's anime community.* Rest of World. https://restofworld.org/2022/ai-backlash-anime-artists/. Accessed 25 Feb 2025.

Deleuze, G., and F. Guattari. 1994. *What is philosophy?* Translated by H. Tomlinson and G. Burchell. Columbia University Press.

Doctorow, C., and R. Giblin. 2022. *Chokepoint capitalism: How big tech and big content captured creative labor markets and how we'll win them back.* Beacon Press.

Drucker, J. 2013. Performative materiality and theoretical approaches to interface. *DHQ: Digital Humanities Quarterly* 7: 1. http://www.digitalhumanities.org/dhq/vol/7/1/000143/000143.html. Accessed 25 Feb 2025.

Engelbart, D. C. 2023. Augmenting human intellect: A conceptual framework. In *Augmented education in the global age*, 13–29. Routledge.

Fazi, M. B. 2019. Can a machine think (anything new)? Automation beyond simulation. *AI & Society* 34:813–824.

Florida, R. 2004. *The rise of the creative class.* Basic Books.

Gadamer, H.G. 2004. *Truth and method*, 2nd, revised edn. Continuum.

Goldman Sachs. 2024. *Generative AI could raise global GDP by 7%.* Goldmansachs.com, May 4. https://www.goldmansachs.com/insights/articles/generative-ai-could-raise-global-gdp-by-7-percent. Access 25 Feb 2025.

Hao, K. 2020. OpenAI is giving microsoft exclusive access to its GPT-3 language model. *MIT Technology Review*, September 23. https://www.technologyreview.com/2020/09/23/1008729/openai-is-giving-microsoft-exclusive-access-to-its-gpt-3-language-model. Accessed 25 Feb 2025.

Hardt, M., and A. Negri. 2000. *Empire.* Harvard University Press.

Harman, G. 2009. *Prince of networks: Bruno Latour and metaphysics.* re.press.

Harvey, D. 2006. *Spaces of global capitalism.* Verso Books.

Kitchin, R. 2017. Thinking critically about and researching algorithms. *Information, Communication & Society* 20 (1): 1–21.

Korten, D. 2001. *When Corporations Rule the World* (2nd ed.). West Hartford: Kumarian Press.

Kubo, R. 2022. *Japan's stagnant wages in the dual labor market*, June 22, 1–36. Ministry of Health, Labour and Welfare.

Langston, J. 2021. From conversation to code: Microsoft introduces its first product features powered by GPT-3. *The AI Blog*, May 25. https://news.microsoft.com/source/features/ai/from-conversation-to-code-microsoft-introduces-its-first-product-features-powered-by-gpt-3/. Accessed 25 Feb 2025.

Latour, B. 2005. *Reassembling the social: An introduction to actor-network-theory.* Oxford University Press Inc.

Lazzarato, M. 2010. The Practice and Anti-dialectical Thought of 'Anartist'. In *Deleuze and Contemporary Art.* Edited by Stephen Zepke & Simon O'Sullivan. Edinburgh: Edinburgh University Press. 100–115.

Luitse, D., and W. Denkena. 2021. The great transformer: Examining the role of large language models in the political economy of AI. *Big Data & Society* 8 (2): 1–14.

Luo, C., S. Li, and T. Sicular. 2020. The long-term evolution of national income inequality and rural poverty in China. *China Economic Review* 62 (101465): 1–15.

Luo, W., and Y. Xie. 2020. Economic growth, income inequality and life expectancy in China. *Social Science & Medicine* 256 (113046): 1–9.

Manovich, L. 2023a. Seven arguments about AI images and generative media. Artificial aesthetics: A critical guide to AI, media and design. *Artificial aesthetics Chapter 5.* https://manovich.net/index.php/projects/artificial-aesthetics. Accessed 25 Feb 2025.

Manovich, L. 2023b. The AI brain in the cultural archive. *Museum of Modern Art Magazine* 2.

Mazzucato, M. 2021. *Mission economy: A moonshot guide to changing capitalism.* Penguin.

McCormack, J. 2023. *The world we made.* Jonmccormack.info. https://jonmccormack.info/project/the-world-we-made. Accessed 25 Feb 2025.

McCormack, J., et al. 2023. Is writing prompts really making art? [Conference session]. In *International conference on computational intelligence in music, sound, art and design (part of EvoStar)*, 196–211. Springer Nature.

McLoughlin, J. 2024. The work of art in the age of artificial intelligibility. *AI & Society*: 1–13.

Milanovic, B. 2020. The world is becoming more equal. *Foreign Affairs*, August 28: 1–7.

Milanovic, B. 2021. *Capitalism, alone: The future of the system that rules the world.* Harvard University Press.

Moruzzi, C. 2022. Creative agents: Rethinking agency and creativity in human and artificial systems. *Journal of Aesthetics and Phenomenology* 9 (2): 1–20.

Moura, L. 2004. *Symbiotic art manifesto 2004.* Leonel Moura website. http://www.leonelmoura.com/symbiotic-art-manifesto/. Accessed 20 Feb 2025.

Moura, L. 2018. Robot art: An interview with Leonel Moura. *Arts* 7 (3): 3–4.

Oosterling, H. 2007. Political art as an interesting gesture? Counter-balancing political fear with artistic inter-esse. In *Citizens and subjects, the Netherlands for example*, ed. Rosi Braidotti, Charles Esche, and M. Maria Hlavajova. BAK (basis for actuele kunst).

Pasquinelli, M. 2023. *The eye of the master: A social history of artificial intelligence.* Verso Books.

Pasquinelli, M., and V. Joler. 2021. The Nooscope manifested: AI as instrument of knowledge extractivism. *AI & Society* 36(4):1263–1280. https://doi.org/10.1007/s00146-020-01097-6.

Pease, A., and S. Colton. 2011. On impact and evaluation in computational creativity: A discussion of the Turing test and an alternative proposal. In *Proceedings of the AISB symposium on AI and Philosophy*, vol. 39.

Pieters, R., and S. Winiger. 2016. *Creative AI: On the democratisation & escalation of creativity.* https://medium.com/@creativeai/creativeai-9d4b2346faf3. Accessed 25 Feb 2025.

Pine, J., and J. Gilmore. 1999. *The experience economy: Work is theatre and every business a stage.* Harvard Business School Press.

Publicis Groupe. 2024. *After another record year Publicis unveils AI strategy*, January 25. https://documents.publicisgroupe.com/events/20240125_Presentation-Unveiling_the_future_of_AI_at_Publicis_Groupe.pdf. Accessed 25 Feb 2025.

Roose, K. 2022. An A.I.-generated picture won an art prize. Artists aren't happy. *New York Times*, September 2. https://www.nytimes.com/2022/09/02/technology/ai-artificial-intelligence-artists.html.

Russel, S., and P. Norvig. 2011. *Artificial intelligence: A modern approach.* 3rd ed. Upper Saddle River: Prentice Hall.

Schopenhauer, A. 1909 [1818]. *The world as will and idea*, Vol. 3. Translated by Haldane, R. B. London: Kegan Paul, Trench, Trübner & Co.

Sennet, R. 2012. *Together: The rituals, pleasures and politics of cooperation.* Yale University Press.

Sennett, R. 2008. *The craftsman.* Yale University Press.

Shen, K., et al. 2022. *The next frontier for AI in China could add $600 billion to its economy.* McKinsey.com, June 7. https://www.mckinsey.com/capabilities/quantumblack/our-insights/the-next-frontier-for-ai-in-china-could-add-600-billion-to-its-economy. Accessed 25 Feb 2025.

Sofokleous, S. 2022. Nonhuman creativity in generative art: Beyond the anthropocentric paradigm. *ISEA2022 BCN Proceedings*: 553–558.

Spencer, D.A. 2024. AI, automation and the lightening of work. *AI & Society*: 1–11.

Statista. 2022. *Hours of video uploaded to YouTube every minute as of February 2022.* Statista.com. https://www.statista.com/statistics/259477/hours-of-video-uploaded-to-youtube-every-minute/. Accessed 1 Feb 2025.

Statista. 2024a. Digital & trends: Video game industry worldwide. *Study*: 1–73. Accessed 10 Feb 2025.

Statista. 2024b. Industries and markets: Advertising worldwide. *Dossier*: 1–48. Accessed 20 Feb 2025.

Still, A., and M. D'Inverno. 2016. A history of creativity for future AI research. In *Proceedings of the seventh international conference on computational creativity*, 147–154.

Tatarkiewicz, W. 1980. *A history of six ideas: An essay in aesthetics.* Translated from the Polish by Christopher Kasparek, The Hague: Martinus Nijhoff; Runco, Mark A.; Albert, Robert S. (2010) "Creativity Research" In Kaufman J. & Sternberg, R. *The Cambridge Handbook of Creativity*, Cambridge University Press.

The Economist Intelligence Unit. 2021. Creative Industries Trade challenges and opportunities post pandemic. *The Economist.* 1–20. https://www.readkong.com/page/creative-industries-trade-challenges-and-opportunities-post-2355445

Triolo, P., and K. Schaefer 2024. China's generative AI ecosystem in 2024. *NBR*, June 27. https://www.nbr.org/publication/chinas-Generative-ai-ecosystem-in-2024-rising-investment-and-expectations/. Accessed 25 Feb 2025.

Van den Akker, P. 2010. *Looking for lines: Theories of the essence of art and the problem of mannerism.* Amsterdam University Press.

Varoufakis, Y. 2023. *Technofeudalism: What killed capitalism.* Random House.

Verschure, P. 2018. The two cultures. In *More than real: Art in the digital age*, ed. Daniel Birnbaum. Koenig.

Vincent, J. 2023. Getty images sues AI art generator stable diffusion in the US for copyright infringement. *The Verge*, February 6. https://www.theverge.com/2023/2/6/23587393/ai-art-copyright-lawsuit-getty-images-stable-diffusion. Accessed 25 Feb 2025.

WPP. 2023. *WPP partners with NVIDIA to build generative AI-enabled content engine for digital advertising.* WPP.com, May 29. https://www.wpp.com/en/news/2023/05/wpp-partners-with-nvidia-to-build-Generative-ai-enabled-content-engine-for-digital-advertising. Accessed 25 Feb 2025.

Zepke, S. 2014. *Art as abstract machine: Ontology and aesthetics in Deleuze and Guattari.* Routledge.

Zylinska, J. 2020. *AI art: Machine visions and warped dreams.* Open humanities press.

CHAPTER 3

Creativity in the Year 2035

Generative AI: The Current State of Play

Before examining future trends, it makes sense to examine some of the issues animating much of the resistance and outright rejection of Gen AI today. The bias that results from the nature of statistical modelling has been earlier mentioned, albeit in passing. We shouldn't underestimate how important training data is to the proper functioning of today's LLMs, including Gen AI. When mentioning the issue of potential biases that comes directly from the statistical distribution of objects in that data, a deeper issue emerged: the issue of objective categorization. Take, for instance, a text-to-image Gen AI like Midjourney. Its training data consists of billions of categorized images. Categorizing objects within an image may seem a straightforward and objective task if we think of things like apples, forks or trains. The reality however is that such categorizations are but a very small fraction of the many ways in which humans use language to talk about the world. In fact, categorizing objects quickly becomes problematic when applied to images of humans.

To see this in practice the example of ImageNet is highly relevant.[1] ImageNet is an image database that has been used for over a decade to

[1] ImageNet is an image database organized according to the WordNet hierarchy (currently only the nouns), in which each node of the hierarchy is depicted by hundreds and thousands of images. The project has been instrumental in advancing computer vision and deep learn-

D. Vargas-Gomez, *The AI Revolution*,
https://doi.org/10.1007/978-3-032-01172-5_3

train and test AI systems. All of the images in the database have been labelled and categorized by humans. The type of labels used on ImageNet goes from unproblematic ones like trumpeter or tennis player to offensive ones like spastic or redneck. The many labels used to classify images result in a highly complex architecture that seems clear and objective at first, yet is ultimately revealed to be deeply offensive, given the way in which it associates certain images of people with labels like loser or slut among many others. No matter how neutral a category may seem, it can always distort the meaning of an image through labels that are gendered, racialized, ableist and ageist. ImageNet is a perfect example of the consequences of categorization, and the belief that labelling people as if they were objects is a straightforward, unproblematic task. Researcher Kate Crawford and artist Trevor Paglen argue this issue has not been resolved by newer models and add it "has only become more common in recent years, often inside the big AI companies, where there is no way for outsiders to see how images are being ordered and classified" (Crawford and Paglen 2019). Could we not just think of a way to classify people that avoids any qualifier or value judgement? Crawford and Paglen's answer is this: no system of classification is free of politics; there is simply no neutral or apolitical perspective that training data can be built upon. Any collection and classification of images is itself a form of politics and censorship or removal of certain terms doesn't resolve the issue. Both classification and removal are political interventions. Addressing "who gets to decide what images mean and what kinds of social and political work those representations perform" is a minefield (Crawford and Paglen). It is thus not a technical issue about finding the right method of classification, but ultimately an issue about the nature of language, its structure and the way we use it.

A commonsense view of language sees it as nothing other than a system of representation and classification. This view sees language as a neutral medium that humans use to transmit information. The idea is simple. Imagine two people standing over an empty field. One of the persons points towards an object in the horizon and utters the word "tree". The other is able to imagine a "tree" and identify the object being pointed out and reply meaningfully by asking, "Do you mean that pine tree?" A clear and simple exchange. Yet, to make that simple example work, many things have been already assumed. It's assumed that both interlocutors knew

ing research. The data is available for free to researchers for non-commercial use (Stanford Vision Lab 2021).

what the meaning of pointing towards something is. It's assumed that both speak the same language and also that the interlocutors were not standing in front of a forest that would make the whole exchange rather odd. Perhaps most obvious is the fact that humans rarely communicate with each other through single-word utterances. This means, in other words, that to make this example work it had to be transformed into a caricature of sorts, all intended to present language as a neutral medium. Many conceptual artists have in fact explored the nature of using language for classification in illuminating ways. One of them was René Magritte. Magritte painted, for instance, an image of an apple with the words "this is not an apple", or a pipe, with the words "this is not a pipe". At first glance the whole thing may seem absurd. It may even give us a bit of discomfort. After all, if that painted apple is not an apple, then what is it? We probably feel the need to inspect the object closely, trying to find clues that confirm the statement "this is not an apple" is actually true. What Magritte's work does is point out something quite obvious: a painted apple is, in fact, not an apple, and the same goes for a painted pipe. Magritte makes us realize that the knee-jerk reaction "this is absurd" or "this makes no sense" is the result of a high level of abstraction in the way we use language, and that we are so used to it that we don't even notice it. The initial presupposition that language is an objective medium is dispelled. By showing how easy it is for ambivalence in language to surface, Magritte lifts the air of objectivity that often accompanies any attempts at objective or scientific classification. We can extrapolate these conclusions to the issue of classification of images in a database like ImageNet. Imagine you are supervising a person who is tasked with labelling images of men of all ethnicities, but of different ages. You decide to check their day's work and find that all images of white men contain the label "beta" and half of those also contain the label "winner". Your employee has already left so you are left alone to decipher how the term beta can coexist with the term winner. At first you think it would just make more sense to use the label alpha when also using the label winner. Later, however, you wonder if perhaps this employee was not really paying a lot of attention to their work. After all, classifying images is not that exciting and can easily get boring fast. You may even begin to think that maybe this employee is a bit of a troll and is trying to mess up your nice system of classification. The next day, after a whole night unable to reach a definitive conclusion, you ask the employee for an explanation, and they tell you that for him the association between beta and winner is completely logical. Through a seemingly well-thought argument your employee explains that males that embrace feminine qualities are much more equipped to live in highly urbanized societies where cooperation and communication are essential to success. Therefore, beta males are winners. However, he adds, some betas dress poorly, so he preferred not labelling them as winners. Is his classification wrong?

The classification may still feel arbitrary, yet my point is not to justify it, but rather to show that creating arbitrary associations between an image and a label is a very human thing. The connection between a referent (an actual apple), an image (a painted apple) and a label (apple) follows no clear objective patterns. The use of labels in our daily lives may be the result of tradition, societal norms or our lived experience, but it's never the result of some objective system that everyone would unquestionably accept.

The problem of classification is, hence, neither a problem of quality nor a problem of consistency. It's a problem of politics, of negotiation and consensus; what we consider a neutral label today may end up becoming offensive in the future or its meaning may simply change with time. Still, prior to the classification of data, the generation of the data itself is anything but problem free. Data protection and privacy concerns are not trivial and are likely to persist, given the vast amount of data that AI systems need for their training to be effective. Gen AI is trained on massive amounts of data from the Internet that are likely to include copyrighted data, often without authorization of the rights-owners. Whether this is permissible is being discussed across jurisdictions, with numerous court cases under way (Zirpoli 2023). The way in which the training data is processed raises complex legal challenges, given the black box nature of neural networks, processes which humans often don't understand and cannot replicate. Clear rules regarding compensation to data owners aren't as straightforward solution either. Firms that either buy the rights away from authors or allow for compensation in the form of royalties to be set up run quickly into trouble. An AI-generated image cannot be easily tracked in most cases to one specific author and issues emerge when comparing an image product of a single prompt that one may result from hundreds of iterations. Despite the complexity, the use of unlicensed content in training data, potential copyright, patent and trademark infringement of AI creations as well as ownership questions around AI-generated works are already significant. Legal decisions that will emerge in the coming years will set precedents and affect the ability of AI companies to train larger and more advanced models. Moreover, intellectual property rights differ among the various legal systems that exist across the globe, resulting in an equally disparate treatment of Al-generated works (Murray 2023). Today, most jurisdictions seem to agree that works generated by Gen AI are not copyrightable (Craig 2021). This precedent resulted, for instance, in the US Copyright Office refusing to register Jason Allen's *Théâtre D'opéra Spatial*, arguing that the process of prompting does not grant authorship over the generated work.[2] This is especially relevant given how important prompting is in the process of using AI systems to augment human creativity. An even deeper and more interactive prompting process will make sense for most creators as long as they are able to claim at least some, if not all, of the property rights of any work produced. The argument espoused by the US court however seems to assume that the creative process is happening within the neural network itself, which is deeply problematic: believing creativity occurs deep within a neural network is like assuming that human creativity happens deep within the brain (McLoughlin 2024, p. 4). As argued earlier, both assumptions are wrong and take us back to the idea of creativity being a talent. They ignore or even erase the creative process, making it a mental process, where reference to any historical and social context is lost. The decision, furthermore, makes no reference to the training data used by Midjourney, which confirms a lack of understanding about how LLMs work.

In the UK, the situation seems to be going in a separate direction, given that under UK copyright law a photograph of an artwork is considered a copy of that work, no matter whether it lives in physical or digital form (McLoughlin, p. 4). Yet, the UK Copyright, Designs and Patents Act 1988 does address computer-generated works adding " 'computer-generated', in relation to a work, means that the work is generated by computer in circumstances such that there is no human author of the work" (McLoughlin, p. 5). This perspective makes autonomy the key aspect to consider. Still, under this view the output of Moura's artbot-made paintings could be arguably seen as computer-generated in the UK, while in the US it doesn't fulfil those criteria, given the need for human prompting. Overall, what these specific cases show is that copyright issues

[2] In its decision the board argued that "the prompting process may involve creativity, but this does not mean that providing text prompts to Midjourney (even if in a large number as 624 revisions and text prompts) "actually forms the generated images" (Stein 2023).

will require compromise and acknowledgement of conflicting interests.[3] The case of music production and composition with the aid of AI is illustrative too. Current LLMs can be trained on music from a specific creator. The AI system may become so proficient at copying this creator's style that it may be able to generate new songs that are stylistically indistinguishable from the musician in question. This means that AI can be effectively used to basically appropriate the style of existing artists. The owner of the system can then claim intellectual property rights over the music style. This ends up in a shocking scenario for the original creator: whenever they make a new song and try to commercialize it, they can potentially be charged with copyright infringement. Sounds far-fetched? Musician and content creator *Venus Theory* (2024) described his own experience at length on his YouTube channel.

It's not hard to imagine that a similar thing could potentially happen to writers or designers, who also tend to develop a personal style with time. In creative areas like music, where style is especially relevant, compensating creators whose music has been used to train AI models is fundamental for musicians, composers and sound engineers to be open and feel comfortable using AI systems. Why would they be hesitant to use the tool, even when it hasn't been trained with their own music? Because it opens the door for the possibility that by using an AI system, they may also be appropriating the music style of other artists, becoming liable themselves of possible infringement. There are no simple answers to the type of issues raised. It's also not my intent to present an expert's view on the topic of regulation, but rather to show how quickly small issues of ownership can snowball into larger questions that transcend legal frameworks, which tend to operate at a national level, requiring instead a global approach, which is currently lacking. As more legal precedent takes shape, however, it's clear that copyright-related decisions have the potential of seriously

[3] McLoughlin (2024) sums this up arguing, "Copyright law, particularly in the digital age, represents more of a compromise between conflicting interests than an endpoint in the discussion about artistry and ownership, but nevertheless represents a valuable launching-off point for critiquing the notion of artistic work in the digital age. The Copyright, Designs and Patents Act 1988 makes clear that the artist has the 'moral right' to be cited and compensated appropriately if their original artwork is represented almost anywhere. It is also the 'moral right' of an artist to protect the integrity and reputation of their work by preventing unauthorised copying in any format. The Act thus restricts secondary representations: if a photograph of an artwork appears in a film, then copyright of the image remains with the original artist (Copyright, Designs and Patents Act 1988)" (p. 5).

impacting the future of LLMs and, specifically to the interest of this text, the future of augmented creativity as a viable avenue for the collaboration between humans and AI systems.

At the heart of discussions around intellectual property ownership lies a flawed understanding of AI: the assumption that the capability of Gen AI to generate relevant responses to a prompt is a sign of knowledge, while the prompting itself is a matter of technique or at best craftsmanship. The earlier discussion about the statistical nature of neural networks and their uncanny ability to generate multidimensional associations between objects makes evident by now that such a process, while complex, does not constitute learning or knowledge in the sense of having an understanding about a topic. If we ask ChatGPT to explain to us the nature of the Vietnam War it will provide us with a relevant and likely accurate answer about the conflict, yet ChatGPT doesn't know what war is, the role of Vietnam's colonial history on its participants or the effect that the Cold War had in escalating the war. All these things are what constitute knowledge. However, the argument doesn't end there. The way we understand knowledge today is very much affected by the mainstream understanding of intelligence that sees it as something that is free of ambivalence. Intelligence is seen as determined by our biology (our genes even) and often reduced to metrics like IQ. Measurements like IQ don't of course measure knowledge, but rather cognitive proficiency against a series of specific tasks, like logical reasoning. When we talk about knowledge, we are talking about a process that is much more social and political than biological (Pasquinelli 2023, p. 235).

To grasp why knowledge is social in nature let's take the work of a civil engineer, for example. Works of civil engineering can be safely traced back to Roman times, to Ancient Greek times and even further back in time. An engineer entering the workforce today mobilizes knowledge about materials, resistance and designs that have accumulated for centuries. Engineers today are biologically the same as engineers a couple of thousand years ago. If an engineer today has more knowledge than one in Roman times, this has little to do with superior genes. Moreover, the example of a civil engineer is anything but unique when we think about knowledge. The fact that trained philosophers still learn about Plato or that Physicists learn about Newton is testimony to the overall importance of knowledge accumulation in any discipline. Even in relatively new disciplines like ICT, knowledge accumulation is fundamental to its progress. We know that in the case of LLMs the data used to train these models is, likewise, much more than information: it's knowledge. When, for instance, an AI system is trained on the literary works of Fitzgerald, Faulkner and Dostoyevsky, these are not simply pieces of information that gain value only after being processed by a neural network. The work of such figures is itself a testament of the accumulation of knowledge; Fitzgerald's work is influenced by authors like Mark Twain, Henry James and John Keats. Our use of AI systems should, therefore and to restate, not simply be reduced to the use of a shiny new tool or gadget, but as the continuation of that process of accumulation. As Pasquinelli (2023) states, the process that led to AI "is a systematic mechanisation and capitalization of collective knowledge [...] into the data sets, algorithms, and statistical models of machine learning, among other techniques" (p. 94).

Lastly, given the iterative nature of prompting and the ability of neural networks to learn from its interactions with users, the creative processes that incorporate AI systems also contribute to this social accumulation of knowledge. This accumulation, it's worth adding, is unique, since we are referring to models that are trained on the entirety of the public Internet, which, without too much hyperbole, contains most of human knowledge to date. The private ownership of these AI systems risks privatizing the benefits of this greater accumulation of knowledge. Past, present and future creators are fundamental to its functioning and to the improvement of today's AI systems, which makes it a vested interest of firms like OpenAI to maintain an active user base of creators. Fairness in relation to the distribution of benefits (property rights) is essential for these systems to continue improving. However, this is not something that can be taken for granted, given Neoliberalism's pressure for short-term gains, even at the expense of the long term. For Pasquinelli and Joler (2021), the long-term risk of bypassing the social nature of knowledge goes beyond the financial rewards, and can be summed up as the risk of allowing private interests to ultimately legislate social behaviour:

> AI easily extends the 'power of normalisation' of modern institutions, among others bureaucracy, medicine and statistics [...] The institutional norm has become a computational one: the classification of the subject, of bodies and behaviours, seem no longer to be an affair for public registers, but instead for algorithms and datacentres. (p. 1275)

The text has talked extensively about the role that the Creative Class plays in challenging the skewed character of LLMs, where stereotypes and clichés are the norm. If we take this argument to its logical conclusion, it's easy to see that unless these systems are constantly challenged, through new data and iterative interactions, their natural tendency is to feature the average, the mainstream and the *normal*. Legislating social behaviour is not a new thing. Philosopher Michel Foucault is well known for his analysis of institutions, and he argued that, for instance, in early modern France, the power of statistics was already being used to measure social norms, and to discriminate between normal and abnormal behaviour (Foucault 2004, p. 26). Extrapolating to the case of AI this means that the normative power of AI in the coming decade and beyond must be questioned along these lines: how will complex patterns frame collective knowledge, and how will its vector spaces and statistical distributions of social behaviours impact what is deemed normal?[4]

Social Futurology

Discussions about any type of future scenario are often motivated by utopian hopes or concerns about apocalyptic dystopian visions. This section will, however, address the topic of futurology from as pragmatic a perspective as possible. It will avoid, for example, assumptions about the inevitable arrival of Artificial General Intelligence (AGI). Current AI systems are not akin to AGI and, presuming that they are, entail precisely the kind of speculation that is sensible to avoid, although a few words on the subject, given its weight on popular culture, are warranted. It remains true that there is no way to fully empty discussions about the future from some degree of speculation. To remain as pragmatic as possible the text will focus on the state of AI systems today and what we know are potential avenues from development. It will, likewise, keep the previously discussed socioeconomic context in mind, to avoid conclusions that extricate technological development from economic reality.

This type of discussion about the future used to fall under the domain of developmental studies, where alternatives to the economic system would be analysed along with plausible scenarios. International Development Consultant David Lempert (2014) argued that development studies are dead in the sense that today no real alternative to the

[4] Pasquinelli argues, "[t]he project of AI has never been truly *biomorphic* (aiming to imitate natural intelligence, as mentioned earlier) but implicitly *sociomorphic*—aiming to encode the forms of social cooperation and collective intelligence in order to control them [...] it was ultimately the self-organization of the social mind that gave form and momentum to the project of AI" (p. 160).

current economic and political systems is presented or even explored.[5] If no alternative is envisioned, the result is that any discussion about the future always presupposes the continuity of the current economic system, that is, the continuity of Neoliberalism as today's hegemonic form of that system.[6] As philosopher Slavoj Zizek famously said, it's easier to imagine the end of the world than the end of capitalism. Hastiness in labelling any alternative as necessarily utopian should give us some pause. The inertia of development along a single path (Neoliberalism) holds sway on our ability to imagine different futures, as attested, for instance, by the uncritical acceptance of higher productivity as a necessarily positive outcome. Imagination is a thought crime, wrote Orwell in *1984*.

Why is it so difficult to envision a different future? Francis Fukuyama's *The End of History,* published shortly after the dissolution of the Soviet Union, was highly influential in presenting Neoliberalism's conquest of the globe as inevitable, albeit shrouded by the promises of liberal democracy. It didn't just shut down the search for economic alternatives but also transformed the future into a rather uniform and predictable affair. Globalization and liberal democracy became the only game in town. While the chosen scope of this study extends only towards the next decade, it will still not simply assume the inevitable continuation of Neoliberalism's recipe of further deregulation and the ever-greater globalization of labour and capital. This perspective is consistent with a pragmatic approach, if we consider key events in our recent history of the too-big-to-fail phenomenon and the bank bailouts that characterized the 2008 financial crisis, the economic consequences of the Covid pandemic, whose fiscal stimulus and nationalist agendas were at loggerheads with most tenets of Neoliberalism, as well as the development of so-called Big Tech, whose debt-powered growth, argues Yanis Varoufakis (2023), signals a fading Neoliberalism, making way for a new type of system he calls Technofeudalism. These profound events show we are already living through a period of transition,

[5] Lempert (2014) adds "there is little or not literature offering competing visions of alternative futures that can be tested that would fulfil aspirations of development [...] [t]he few alternative visions of "sustainability" or "steady state" that challenge (or regulate) the agenda for growth, seem more designed to head off inevitable destruction and calamity than to offer a positive alternative vision" (p. 224).

[6] "The agenda for such studies seems to be set by powerful political and economic actors in concert. [...] Challenges to this globalization agenda seem to be disempowering critiques that reinforce its inevitability or simply calls for more funding or more attention to specific interests" (Lempert 2014, p. 224).

where clashing economic interests are likely to speed up or hinder the development of AI.

Furthermore, social futurology should not presume that a system can function independently from its participants, which would assume that it can only be af-fected by external forces. It must instead take into account feedback loops and potential internal forces of change. After all, even intellectuals shaping the zeitgeist, like Yuval Noah Harari, refer to the era in which we live in as the *Anthropocene*, where "one biological species, *Homo sapiens*, has become a major agent in shaping the natural circumstances of its own existence. The future will "upgrade humans into gods, and turn Homo sapiens into Homo deus"" (Shapin 2017, p. 2). A future where AI systems have been incorporated into the entirety of our social life, like how smartphones or social media networks have done in the past decades, cannot, thus, be seen as independent from the economic system that spawned them. On the contrary, feedback loops between AI adoption and the ability of industries to adapt will shape the future development of the technology and whether the social tensions of today will be exacerbated or ameliorated. Likewise, the possible pathways of development that countries can follow may be equally narrowed or widened by the generalized adoption of AI, or by the diffusion of the technology within certain industries over others.

Lastly, we must recognize that the tension that exists between technological determinism and free will complicates matters further. This tension has animated both the fears and the hopes of past technological developments and is especially relevant with regard to AI. Ideological interpretations of technological development usually attempt to circumvent this tension by rhetorical means. A libertarian interpretation of technological determinism can present AI systems as a liberatory force for good and a steppingstone towards a utopian and stateless society. The trope of this interpretation of technological development is to equate technological development with innovation, understood as a process that requires cooperation among free individuals. For libertarians and free-market advocates, only humans who are free from external coercion (e.g. the state, the legal framework, supranational institutions like the UN, etc.) can generate innovation. Freedom is their ultimate goal and motivation, because progress can only result from free-acting individuals. Innovation becomes, in turn, the concrete way to solve any problems the future may bring; problems are best solved by allowing free markets to operate, not by planning for desirable outcomes. Under this interpretation, the existence of AI systems themselves is, hence, confirmation that at least in certain parts of the globe (Silicon Valley or the US) people live free from coercion. Innovation is therefore the result of living in a free society and technological progress always acts as a positive force. This makes the study of alternatives or future scenarios unnecessary and even potentially harmful. Such view, for instance, animates OpenAI's (2018) charter, which states: "[Our] mission is to ensure that artificial general intelligence (AGI)—by which we mean highly autonomous systems that outperform humans at most economically valuable work—benefits all of humanity".

This type of technological determinism that is equated with freedom is certainly not free from criticism. Never mind, for instance, that China, hardly a stateless society, is a player that stands on equal footing with the Silicon Valley crowd when it comes to technological development and AI. However, just as a libertarian view can lead to uncritical adoption of any new technology, fear of technology can make us equally short-sighted. Harari (2017) projects a future of data controlled by algorithms and artificial intelligence, finding the possibility that "dataism threatens to do to Homo sapiens what Homo sapiens has done to all other animals" (p. 460). Technological determinism is for him a gateway towards our impending doom. Despite the popularity of his ideas, Harari's alarmism may fail to sway people, because it appears to ignore that algorithms and machine learning are very much part of people's lives today. Concerns about data privacy, among others, are no small change, but they certainly don't feel as threatening as the upcoming extinction of the human species. In fact, it's reasonable for anyone to conclude that if machine learning and AI algorithms are already part of our lives today, then perhaps the future is likely to simply be a slightly more advanced version of the present.[7] In a way, Harari's claims feel more as an indictment of the world as it is today than a serious picture of what the near future may look like.[8] Harari's own bias

[7] This point is made too by Lev Manovich, who argues, "already today many of us rely on AI 'to automate our aesthetic choices (via recommendation engines)' or even engage in aesthetic production (e.g. by relying on algorithms embedded in our mobile phones' software to produce professional-looking photos with great ease)" (Zylinska 2020, p. 146).

Zylinska, J. (2020). AI art: machine visions and warped dreams. Open humanities press.

[8] For Shapin (2017) Harari assumes the future will be a clear continuation of the present, concluding that "[u]nless there is secure information suggesting otherwise, the weather tomorrow will probably resemble the weather today; next winter will be colder than next autumn; marathon times will continue to get lower; and, in technology, computing power will get cheaper, as will the cost of photovoltaic cells. These aren't certain bets, but they're good ones ... What can't be imagined can't be predicted" (p. 6).

can be summed up in the claim that "[h]umanity's future is in the hands of technical experts—in biotechnology, artificial intelligence, cognitive and computer science" (Shapin 2017, p. 4). In reality, this same sentence will be read by some as a positive conclusion rather than a bad omen. Technocracy is hardly a new thing, and the same goes for computer science. However critical we may be about our world today, the jump from today's algorithm-filled Internet to human extinction is still a highly speculative one and a leap that most people will simply not take.

So, where to begin? Copenhagen's Business School doctoral student Kristian D'Amato (2024) sums up in a convenient way the conditions of possibility that allowed AI systems to emerge and which are likely to shape its future in the coming decade.

> (1) a deeply connected society where information is not only privileged, but where all the modalities of expression must necessarily be disseminated through connective technology, (2) a dominant ethos of self-disclosure, (3) a strongly reductionist, dataist scientific ideology, (4) an entrenched humanism in constant tension with biopower, reflected in the strategies of states and private companies alike, and (5) a late-capitalist economy where information is commodified and human intelligence is in the process of being so. (p. 6)

While Chap. 2 of this book surveyed the economic conditions under which current AI systems came to life, the points raised by D'Amato help us take it a step further. It's worth noting on his first point that, not only is connectivity, whether through social media, instant messaging platforms or the like, essential to the rapid adoption of AI systems, but, perhaps more importantly, that connectivity has changed the nature of how we spend our lives. The advent of the Internet didn't simply add a new means to communicate with family, friends and acquaintances. It did much more than that. The Internet has become the space where we spend half of our lives. Whether for work or leisure, being online has become a ubiquitous experience and to a high extent the main avenue through which we learn about the world. The Internet didn't add hours to the day for us to spend online but rather replaced much of the time we used to spend offline. Just like the data LLMs get trained on makes up their entire worldview, so has the worldview of many millions of humans been shaped by the Internet. Millions of so-called Millennials, Gen Zs and Gen Alphas don't simply use or enjoy the Internet, but their worldviews have been moulded by it.[9] AI is likely to play an even greater role in shaping the worldview of future generations as it becomes more and more accessible. The culture of self-disclosure mentioned by D'Amato is closely connected with his first point. That ubiquitous connectivity comes at the extent of our privacy is barely news today, but the extent to which that can impact people's lives has always been obfuscated by technical jargon and an overall acceptance that if you have nothing to hide, you have nothing to fear. Machine learning algorithms already know us better than we know ourselves, as anyone browsing through Amazon, YouTube, TikTok or any other social media platform knows first-hand. We've also all become used to targeted ads coming our way as soon as we visit a Website or search something on Google. Yet, with AI's hunger for data this may go even further, as the arising tensions around intellectual property rights discussed above clearly show. A scenario where we all must accept that the price to pay for the convenience of using AI systems is to allow them to gobble up our online lives is one that will be played out in the coming decade.

Lastly, some additional words on his fourth point are warranted: a humanism in tension with bio-power (modes of control) and the interest of both states and private firms alike. There are a few aspects to unpack here. Chapter 1 analysed the ways in which humanism has often led to a narrow view of creativity, centred around the individual. Chapter 2 argued this is a perspective that is often supported by meritocracy's emphasis on individual rewards for equally individual talent. At the same, the incorporation of AI systems into our lives can also take us on a path of divergence, where certain individuals reap the benefits of AI, while others are left behind. While it seems implausible today that a company like OpenAI would want only certain people to use Chat GPT, that assumption may be mistaken. The costs of increasing the power and capabilities of current LLMs will lead to a price point that many people simply may not be able to afford. It's entirely plausible that a tier system sets in, one where only a few wealthy individuals have access to the latest models, while the vast majority resign to using smaller and to a certain extent outdated versions,

[9] Zylinska (2020) states in this regard that "[t]he belief in the wisdom of the crowd associated with the optimism of the early internet era, and driven by the spirit of communitarianism and collaboration, has lost its shine in the age of global digital surveillance, fake news, Twitter bubbles and the possible election manipulation via social media. The crowd has now been revealed to be not so much wise as mouldable and subject to all sorts of exploitation" (p. 125).

or perhaps to using ad-supported versions of AI. This means that the development of future AI systems will most likely be guided by the interests of only certain groups, but it won't stop there. Such separation may do more harm than simply exacerbating economic inequality—which is no small thing, to be sure. The real risk however is that it may create divergent pathways that within the span of only a few decades could result in a fundamental split among human groups. Tiered AI systems may create big divides among society, where only a privileged few will have access to opportunities that allow them to enjoy a dramatically higher quality of health, leisure and education, among others.

The next sections will further discuss how these forces impact creativity and the Creative Class, by analysing three specific tendencies and the potential scenarios linked to them in the coming decade. However, a brief digression into the subject of AGI is still pertinent. While no current AI system can be labelled as AGI, AGI futurology has been fundamental in fashioning the narratives that define both utopian and dystopian visions of AI. While billions have not had the chance to use a system like ChatGPT or Midjourney, they are still likely to have some idea about AGI. AGI has been a defining part of popular culture for many decades, from Kubrick's Machiavellian HAL9000 to Spike Jonze's affectionate AI in the movie *Her*, just to name two examples, separated by fifty years of history. We live in an era where drastically opposite visions about AI coexist, disclosing perhaps some fundamental fears about the nature of technology and our inability to take control over an uncertain future. This uncertainty is not a fact of life, but the product of Neoliberalism's faith in markets and the inability or unwillingness of state and corporate interests to envision together the shared future that we can build with the help of AI.

Modernism, AGI and Transhumanism

How does societal progress come about? What is the role of technology in making progress possible? It's been argued that in today's world progress and technology often appear to us inextricably linked. This seemingly natural link dresses technology as both desirable and a necessary aspect in the improvement of our living conditions. Improvements in medicine during the nineteenth and twentieth centuries, for instance, reduced infant mortality to a fraction of what it used to be and overall led to longer and healthier lives. This is, however, not the full story. The link between technological development and the appearance of ever more destructive weapons, unforeseen biological hazards and the destruction of ecosystems is equally relevant and complicates the positive view of technology, revealing it as one-sided. The reality, hence, is that technology is anything but a neutral aspect of our lives and of human history. Technological development is loaded with value statements that are constantly reflecting the strong tensions that underpin it. This section will further explore the way in which narratives about technology attempt to articulate, ignore or erase those tensions. It will show as well how omitting these tensions creates an opening for political viewpoints that not only support technological progress, but also make it seem inevitable. Postures that strip the conversation from intellectual nuance push any conversation about the future into dogmatic camps: either uncritical advocacy that makes it inseparable from progress or irrational fears, based on it being counter to our human nature. Especially relevant to the subject of AI is the idea of *Singularity* that informs the notion of Artificial General Intelligence (AGI); few ideas cause as much hopes as they do fears as the emergence of AGI does today.[10]

When it comes to creativity few people encapsulate the idea of societal progress being inextricably linked to technology like poet and art theorist Filippo Marinetti. Marinetti's *Futurist Manifesto* was first published in the French newspaper *Le Figaro*, where he made an unapologetic call for a clean break with the past:

> To admire an old picture is to pour our sensibility into a funeral urn instead of casting it forward with violent spurts of creation and action. Do you want to waste the best part of your strength in a useless admiration of the past, from which you will emerge exhausted, diminished, trampled on? (Marinetti 2009)

Marinetti excoriated virtually all ideas that would see value in the past: tradition, custom and heritage were ballast that needed to be let go. He celebrated, in turn, the courage and audacity of those who were willing and unafraid to revolt against them. For Marinetti, art was necessarily future looking, and any reminder of the past would do little more than hinder its progress. Technological development played for Marinetti a key

[10] A quick glance at the depictions of AGI in popular culture reveal the continuous presence of these opposite points of view in our social imaginary: from *2001: A Space Odyssey* to *Blade Runner*, *Terminator* and *The Matrix*, which depict the fundamentally negative nature of AGI to the benevolent depictions found in movies like *Wall-e*, *Star Trek*, *Star Wars* and *Transformers*.

role in forcing societies to critically reckon with their past, pushing them to envision a future of new social constructs: new institutions, new laws, new identities. But how influential were Marinetti's ideas really? Media researcher John Potts (2018) goes as far as to claim that Marinetti invented futurism: "a worldview perpetually geared to the glories of things yet to come" (p. 104). Marinetti's ideas gave in a way meaning to the term avant-garde, transforming it into both an attitude towards the future and a continuous challenge of the past. This expectation of the future is fully reflected in our daily use of the term *modern*, which remains today a celebration of the new and of things and ideas that can only take place when we embrace change.

Marinetti's ideas gave a voice, within the space of art and creativity, to a newfound love for technology and for machines. He made this love for the future synonymous with a youthful spirit: "When we are forty let younger and stronger men than we throw us in the wastepaper basket like useless manuscripts!" (Marinetti 2009). He was eager for the people of his time to leave behind the past as well as the fear about an uncertain future. Marinetti's attitude towards the future and towards the impact of technology, however, wasn't naive, in the sense of simply painting it as noble and harm-free (Potts 2018, p. 104). On the contrary, he embraced the brutal side of technological development, the destructive elements that came along with it: "Beauty exists only in struggle. There is no masterpiece that has not an aggressive character. Poetry must be a violent assault on the forces of the unknown, to force them to bow before man" (Marinetti 2009). Marinetti's ideas resonate in important ways with many of the arguments made about the work-public encounter in Chap. 1. They are relevant to the dynamic of deterritorialization and reterritorialization theorized by Deleuze and Guattari, and emphasize the role that novelty plays in the systems' thinking approach to creativity. It was argued, in particular, that challenging past ideas is fundamental for relevant novelty to emerge and for creative networks to subsist. An important distinction however, as the many examples discussed throughout this text showed, is that the notion of creativity proposed here is not a full rejection, but a challenge to the authority and relevance of dominant paradigms. From the perspective of creativity, it is a creation of the new, based on the old, rather than a rejection of the old full stop.[11] Notwithstanding, Marinetti is right in

[11] This view is shared by Manovich (2023a) when claiming that "modern art developed by reinterpreting and copying images and forms from old art traditions, such as Japanese prints (van Gogh), African sculpture (Picasso), and Russian icons (Malevich)" (p. 6).

saying that breaking with the past requires courage and a certain attitude of revolt. A key question is, hence, how is this attitude reflected, if at all, in the expectations about future AI systems?

Marinetti's ideas reflect the logic of *Modernism* in the arts. Modern artists wanted to depart from classical art, from a canon that emphasized narrative content over form, providing clear hierarchies to the different visual elements of composition. Simply put, "their art was founded on a fundamental rejection of everything that had come before it" (Manovich 2023a, p. 5). At a first glance modernism seems to be the opposite of what training an LLM entails: "Neural networks are trained [...] by learning from historical culture and art created up to now. A neural network is analogous to a very conservative artist studying in the "meta" "museum without walls" that houses historical art" (Manovich, p. 5). Along these lines, one of the main features of today's Gen AI is precisely its inability to challenge or think beyond the data it has been trained on. Not only is it unable to challenge dominant ideas and categories, but it amplifies them even further. We must, therefore, not lose sight of the fact that even if AI systems are cutting-edge technology, we cannot assume that their adoption challenges the dominant paradigms or advances the ideas of progress that modernism and Marinetti embraced.

How can this cutting-edge technology be both a sign of progress and of stagnation? The answer seems to lie on a phenomenon that is unique to our age of computers and that is the divorce between pursuing technological development and pursuing societal change. This is the belief social reality can be immune to the introduction of new and often revolutionary technologies. It's better encapsulated as the belief that pursuing technological change should not threaten the social order in significant ways. This is different from Marinetti's own perspective, which saw in technological development a necessary force that would bring about societal change. Marinetti's love of machines came from a place of hope in the possibility of social change and shouldn't be reduced to an odd fascination with steel, cogs and moving parts. Machines, he thought, were a threat to the dominant ideas and institutions of the time. Today we find ourselves surrounded by narratives about technological development that are, on the contrary, fully supportive of the current social order. Change and disruption are often presented as entirely compatible with Neoliberalism, where the only shift is which market is created, and which market is destroyed. It's, no doubt, true that destroying a market, like the market for typewriters, had serious consequences to those involved. Still, such events usually remain trapped within the logic of the market. In the case of typewriters, the harm perceived is the loss of income to those involved, not the loss of the knowledge needed to make typewriters or the loss of books that will no longer be made using typewriters. This makes minor corrections the best course of action; a program that retrains and provides new employment to those who lost it would do the trick. In no way would such a solution challenge Neoliberalism. Unlike Marinetti's perspective, technological development is no longer seen as a wild space that contains the seeds for new and better futures, some of which may be barely imagined today. In a nutshell, today's narratives often defang technological development. The stories created to justify it domesticate its impact on society. This is why McKinsey and Goldman Sachs can safely predict that AI will bring about revolutionary changes to the workplace, without any office worker really believing that an actual revolution is soon to take place.

Perhaps the most notable instance of social futurology on AI, presenting a revolution without revolt, is the idea of the *Singularity*. In 1987, inventor and futurist Ray Kurzweil wrote *The Age of Intelligent Machines*, which he later adapted in a second book called *The Age of Spiritual Machines* (1999). Just a few years later Kurzweil updated both texts into a single volume called *The Singularity Is Near* (2005). The term Singularity can be read as synonymous with AGI. Current AI systems, it bears repeating, are not AGI, and no clear avenue for development exists today that allows us to conclude that LLMs can in the coming decades become AGI (Voss and Jovanovic 2023). Next to this, some researchers also point out to the fact that no current work on Gen AI is part of a roadmap towards AGI and most AI research remains unrelated to the development of AGI.[12] While many of the challenges are often discussed in purely technical terms, a brief and less technical digression on the main challenges that AI researchers and developers currently face is relevant, helping us understand the implications of Kurzweil's futurology.

As discussed earlier, the generative aspect of current systems means that they produce content based on probabilities and correlations. This means, in turn, that "almost all of their knowledge is non-adaptive, not acquired interactively or in real-time" (Voss and Jovanovic, p. 2). Unlike humans, these AI systems cannot update their knowledge based on new

[12] Voss and Jovanovic (2023) state that an "objective measure is whether the AI work done involves a clearly identified step or aspect of an overall detailed plan to achieve AGI. Very little AI work matches this criterion. Specifically, Generative AI research does not" (p. 5).

information and they cannot respond to new situations. Both aspects are necessary milestones on a roadmap towards AGI. Furthermore, current systems are trained on specific types of data and are unable to integrate multiple "modalities", such as images, audio and video simultaneously (Feng et al. 2024, p. 8). To achieve this integration, we need greater transparency about the model's inner workings. Researchers must be able to fully understand how different components of the model contribute, hinder or simply shape the response to specific problems (Feng, T., et al., p. 9). Contrary to images of AGI in popular culture, where its inner workings and machinations are often portrayed as opaque to its human users (e.g. Ava in the movie *Ex Machina*), AGI cannot be a black box. Only a better understanding of current AI's "thought processes" will be able to deliver better data integration, the ability to adapt to new data and the ability to go beyond their current statistical thinking, all prerequisites to achieve AGI. Causation and complex reasoning are fundamental to human thinking and are currently unavailable in even the most advanced LLMs, which today "require strict guidelines, meaning they don't reason but rather follow their programmers' choices" (Feng, T., et al., p. 12). Lastly, current AI systems are still prone to generate content that is inaccurate or nonsensical, in a phenomenon referred to as *hallucination*.[13] These issues

[13] IBM defines hallucinations as "a phenomenon wherein a large language model (LLM)—often a generative AI chatbot or computer vision tool—perceives patterns or objects that are nonexistent or imperceptible to human observers, creating outputs that are nonsensical or altogether inaccurate" (IBM 2024). Pattern recognition is central to machine learning and to the way in which generative AI delivers results based on a human prompt. While mostly seen as an unwanted phenomenon, hallucinations can reveal much about existing biases within the training data as well as potential new avenues for rethinking our own way of approaching and solving problems. While technical in nature, an interesting example from a researcher in the field of psychiatry documenting their interaction with ChatGPT is illustrative of the issue: "I asked which brain regions would be of particular interest in relation to antipsychotic treatment. The thalamus was an unexpected suggestion, so I requested supportive literature. Five references were duly supplied, including publications by established researchers in reputable journals. By this time my level of enthusiasm had risen considerably as new possibilities for the analysis emerged based on these heretofore undiscovered studies. My next step was to source these publications via PubMed. The first reference was to a well-known longitudinal study reporting brain changes over time—but it was inappropriate, as it was not focussed on the thalamus. I was unable to trace three of the four remaining references, whether I searched by author names, manuscript title or journal details. Similarly, with Google Scholar I was not able to identify the articles. Entering the Digital Object Identifier (DOI) number in my searches took me to totally unrelated publications. Becoming increasingly uneasy, I questioned ChatGPT about previous studies whose content I was familiar

pose without a doubt incredible engineering challenges. Suffice it to say here that it's due to such difficulties that many AI researchers remain sceptical about the current technology being able to ever deliver AGI.[14] Why then discuss Kurzweil's ideas or AGI in general? The answer is that Kurzweil has been extremely influential in inspiring the work of firms like OpenAI. They have made AGI a desirable proposition and a business objective worth pursuing. While it remains unlikely that AGI is achieved any time soon, attempts to get there do indeed guide the social futurology around AI. Part of what keeps AGI a north star for industry leaders is that Kurzweil doesn't reduce it to the creation of intelligent machines. The Singularity encompasses the expansion and amplification of our overall human capabilities. Kurzweil advocates for a future without biological limitations. He instead embraces a vision for humanity called *Transhumanism*.[15]

In Kurzweil's vision, humans become many times smarter thanks to biotechnology, and machines become more human thanks to advances in IT infrastructure. According to this view, advancements in neuroscience,

with, including my own, as a test of accuracy. Some of the answers provided were patently incorrect. The problem therefore goes beyond just creating false references. It includes falsely reporting the content of genuine publications. Thus, while most attention to date has focussed on the production of false references as these are the easiest to detect, the veracity of any content inputs provided by ChatGPT cannot be trusted. The cause of these falsifications has been linked to a disturbance in language production, with probabilistic outputs based on estimates of semantic similarity. This allows informed guesses, with bits of false information being mixed with factual information" (Emsley 2023, p. 1).

[14] Researching other paths outside of the transformer-based LLMs of today is, not surprisingly, advocated by AI researchers as a necessary next step: "There is yet no general solution within deep learning to the problem of generalising outside the training space. And it is for that reason that we need to look to different kinds of solutions if we want to reach artificial general intelligence" (Marcus 2018, p. 17).

[15] The term "transhuman" was coined by futurist and science fiction author FM-2030, who used it as a shorthand for "transitory human". His view of a transhuman, though inspired by fiction, is to a high degree comparable to Kurzweil's view, since both look at prostheses, reconstructive surgery and intensive use of telecommunications (van der Vleuten 2014, p. 7). "The term transhumanism was coined in 1957 by Julian Huxley (1887–1975), the grandson of the Victorian Darwinian Thomas Henry Huxley. In his New Bottles for New Wine (1957), Julian Huxley advocated the fulfilment society, which will be committed to the full development of the human potential and will replace the welfare society, the efficient society, or the power society. For Huxley, transhumanism was another word for his "evolutionary humanism," namely, the deliberate effort by mankind to 'transcend itself—not just sporadically . . . but in its entirety, as humanity . . . Man remaining man, but transcending himself, by realizing new possibilities of and for his human nature.'" (van der Vleuten, p. 20).

genomics, robotics, nanotechnology, computers, and artificial intelligence "make it possible to increase human health-span, extend our intellectual and physical capacities, and give us increased control over our own mental states and moods" (Grassie 2011, p. 13).

In a world where humans become cyborgs, our entire experience of the digital world no longer requires screens, as humans will be able to directly connect with computers. Virtual reality will become indistinguishable from physical reality, making the interaction between machines and humans more seamless, while also allowing machines to understand the physical world as well as humans do. After this point, Kurzweil argues, these cyborgs will be able to evolve their intelligence, far surpassing humans, resulting in a separation and evolution of the human species through diverging paths. Those humans who remain as we are today will be relegated to the bins of history or worse. At this point, machines themselves will diverge from their human creators, evolving and improving their capabilities, surpassing today's human intelligence by many orders of magnitude.

At first glance Kurzweil's ideas may seem too fantastic to belong anywhere outside the sci-fi genre. So, how can he be sure that any of these things are possible? He argues that it all comes down to the exponential growth of our available compute. This view of exponential growth is well established within the field of ICT. It's derived from what is called *Moore's Law*. Gordon Moore was the director of research and development at Fairchild Semiconductor in the 1960s. He was concerned with the need to reduce the cost and size of the circuit components used by computers at the time. In 1965 he wrote a paper called "Cramming More Components onto Integrated Circuits", where he made a ten-year prediction about the future of such components (Moore 1998). Moore predicted the doubling every year of the number of components that would be fitted onto an integrated circuit and added that this yearly doubling of capacity would continue into the future. Not really a "law" but an engineering challenge, his predictions held for the coming ten years and beyond that: "by 2015 the Intel chip was thought to cram two billion transistors, spaced 14 nanometres apart, onto a tiny surface" (Potts 2018, p. 109). Moore's Law of exponential growth is, thus, fundamental to Kurzweil ideas on AGI. The extrapolation of Moore's Law onto AGI can be understood as the exponential growth of the AI compute available happening at the same time as the increased efficiency in the volume of training data needed for AI to deliver satisfactory results (results that can at least match those of an average human). According to Kurzweil, "we will have enough hardware to emulate human intelligence with supercomputers by the end of this decade [2020]. Personal computers with the ability to emulate human intelligence will follow a decade later. Effective software models of human intelligence will be available by the mid-2020s" (van der Vleuten 2014, p. 6). Kurzweil (2005) predicts, or better envisions, that by 2045 a threshold event called Singularity will take place (p. 151). When this happens, intelligence will become disembodied, meaning that "future machines will be human even if they are not biological" [...] "This will be the next step in evolution" (Kurzweil, p. 136).

The Singularity is, thus, much more than another sci-fi story about a supercomputer. It's a vision about a future where humanity has been divided in ways that go far beyond the economic inequalities we see today. We should understand the enthusiasm for AGI as enthusiasm for transhumanism. Kurzweil's ideas may be rightly seen today as more sci-fi than science. They help us, among other things, to understand that the development of AGI is interdisciplinary at its core, requiring expertise way beyond hardware and software development, including many subdomains within the fields of neuroscience, genetics, biology and physics. Kurzweil's extrapolation of Moore's Law, nonetheless, appears to conflate biological evolution with technological progress.[16] He sees technological progress as an evolutionary shortcut that would allow humans to compress the extremely long periods of evolutionary change that dictated our past into controllable processes that are shorter than the span of a human lifetime. Moreover, his uncritical reliance on the exponential character of technological progress gives an air of inevitability to the dawn of AGI. His faith in both exponential growth and the desirability of transhumanism narrows all future pathways to the point that no other scenarios are deemed relevant. This inability to even consider other possibilities reveals in his thinking the same type of ideological bias found in Fukuyama's *The End of History*, where Neoliberalism's combination of globalization, free markets and liberal democracy is deemed to be not just desirable, but inevitable. It's the reason why, to repeat, Zizek said it was easier to imagine the end

[16] Grassie (2011) argues Kurzweil's belief in technology as a cure-for-all problems falls into a fallacy of extrapolation: assuming exponential trends (Moore's Law) will continue, ignores physical limits (e.g., quantum tunnelling in chips), and simply replicates capitalist's old logic of extractivism in an age where climate change and a whole host of ecological costs demand better stewardship of our planetary resources (pp. 256–263).

of the world than the end of capitalism. And were we to still have doubts about where Kurzweil stands in relation to the topic, he makes it clear for us on the same book: "I believe that maintaining an open free-market system for incremental scientific and technological progress, in which each step is subject to market acceptance, will provide the most constructive environment for technology to embody widespread human values" (Kurzweil 2005, p. 420). Along these lines Thomas (2024) argues Transhumanists revere the "instrumental potentialities of technology" and yet "fail to…situate technological advancement within the social, economic, cultural and political framework" (p. 6).

In other words, AGI is for Kurzweil and his Transhumanists as inevitable as the economic system from which it emerges. There is of course nothing certain about the development of AGI. However, following Kurzweil could lead us to conclude that, in order to achieve AGI, we must ensure the status quo of the current economic system remains in place. Transhumanism, far from transcending neoliberal capitalism, in fact enshrines its core tenets—deregulation, hyper-individualism, financialization and free-market faith—by treating human life as raw material for endless optimization. Its mindset assumes that every human limitation is a metric, a KPI to be improved. Moreover, the financialization of human enhancement—where Silicon Valley magnates pour billions into life-extension startups, brain–computer interfaces and designer-baby technologies—turns future human capacities into speculative assets (Thomas 2024, p. 21).

Given that from an engineering point of view AGI is still more fiction than reality, what makes this conclusion rather sinister, is the way in which a narrative of revolutionary change is used to actually conceal a conservative agenda in favour of the status quo; transhumanism will be a possibility only for those who can afford it. Transhumanists' enthusiasm for morphological freedom, for the "ability to choose a body we wish to have regardless of birth facts", obscures how only those with capital can afford enhancements, magnifying current economic inequalities under the guise of freedom (Tirosh-Samuelson 2017, p. 271). The logic of morphological freedom follows, in addition, a hedonist imperative, where death and the inability to enjoy life are seen as the main enemies to combat. Human biology is, in practice, seen as an obstacle to overcome as it is the reality of that biology that constrain humans to live to their fullest potential. This is not simply a call to end disease or improve the quality of life of older individuals, which is a goal that many people would agree with. Transhumanist enthusiasm for overcoming biological limits fails to recognize that the emotional and physical realities of human joy are rooted in that same biology. This means that freeing a human from that biology comes at a cost, because it cannot be done without freeing them from all such aspects that make human life worth living: relationships, collaboration, creativity, exploration, etc. These are not just vague or abstract concepts that can be applied to anything and everywhere. Their meaning is directly related to our lived experience. Imagine what it would mean to enter a marriage knowing that it would literally last hundreds of years. Or, imagine what the emotional value of experiencing something new will be, from a new culture in a distant country to a new relationship, if there is a technology that can be used to generate those same emotions without leaving the comfort of your home. Likewise, the value of a learning experience comes also under fire. The discipline, commitment and often collaboration needed to acquire new skills become unnecessary in a Transhumanist world, yet they are fundamental to what it means to be a human today and for hundreds of thousands of years. Hence, from a philosophical point of view a human who is no longer constrained to its biological realities is no longer a human, at least not as we understand human existence today, but something else entirely.[17]

Once we get over its bells and whistles, transhumanism appears as little more than a reactionary ideal that is totally at odds with Marinetti's enthusiasm for the future. It's not miniaturization and semiconductors that make the future of AI an interesting space for analysis and social futurology. For the future of AI to be a truly exciting one, we must allow for the door towards socioeconomic change to remain open.

[17] At the turn of the century, Michael Sandel was already sounding the alarms on the impact of Transhumanism and on the importance of understanding Transhumanism as more than enthusiasm for technology or human enhancement. Genetic engineering, he argues, turns offspring into objects of parental ambition, undermining the unconditional love rooted in accepting the child as given. He writes that enhancement's deepest moral objection is hubris: the parent's "drive to master the mystery of birth", which "would disfigure the relation between parent and child" and deprive parents of the humility and enlarged sympathies cultivated by openness to the unexpected (Sandel 2004). If people come to see talents as fully self-made, the cornerstones of humility and solidarity will weaken: Sandel's point being that removing nature's randomness also removes a basis for empathy and justice. In sum, he contends that genetic mastery risks transforming meritocracy into a harsher hierarchy, eroding the very values (humility, responsibility, solidarity) that justify social cooperation.

Pandora's Box and the Fear of the Future

Just like a vision of technological progress that renders it desirable and inevitable can end up narrowing our horizon, so can a vision that presents technology as fundamentally inhuman and technological progress as suspicious and dangerous. Futurist Alvin Toffler's (1984) *Future Shock* explored these fears, documenting the stress and disorientation that he saw already back then as a product of the "information overload of modern living" (p. 318). The theme of information overload has been a concern of researchers and psychologists for decades and is arguably more relevant today than it was back then (Misra and Stokols 2012, pp. 737–738). The advent of the Internet in a globalized world allows any person with a connection to have access to more information today than was ever possible in Toffler's time.[18] Information overload renders our human limitations transparent: as humans, we are simply unable to deal with large volumes of information and being subjected to it on a regular basis can cause all sorts of mental and physical harm, from chronic anxiety to burnout and even serious mental distress (Misra and Stokols, pp. 752–753). Information overload is but the tip of the iceberg. Toffler argues future shock results from "too much change in too short a period of time" (Toffler 1984, p. 12). People in technologically advanced societies, where such changes happen most rapidly, struggle, in turn, to understand their causes or benefit from them, by adapting to a heightened pace of life (Grassie 2011, p. 239). Technological innovation, therefore, can end up causing negative responses, including fear of the future. Toffler used the term "post-industrial" to refer to the developed economies of his time, following the term's usage by sociologist Alan Touraine. The term is perhaps best known through the work of Daniel Bell in his 1974 book *The Coming of Post-industrial Society*. A post-industrial society is one where most of its urban workforce is engaged in the service sector, whose core is to deal with information at scales that were unprecedented in the industry or agriculture sectors. Toffler warned that future shock is a disease of post-industrial societies that happens when individuals fail to adapt to the accelerating pace of this "roaring current of change" (Toffler 1984, p. 11). The fear of change is, therefore, not simply a fear of an uncertain future, but also and perhaps most relevantly, a resistance to change. We see that

[18] Farhoomand and Druiy (2002) argue already at the turn of the twenty-first century that very high rates of data production, dissemination and storage prompt concerns about the effects of information overload on the ability of people to make decisions.

resistance manifested in the rejection of new technology, but not only then. Resistance to new information, new ideas, new ways of acting and living is also an essential part of that fear of a future. Harari's warnings about AI are an instance of such fear of the future, albeit focused on a rejection of transhumanism as a desirable ideal for human kind. The previous section argued against the desirability of transhumanism. The main concern being that it's a reactionary idea that delivers no meaningful change, which is an argument not found in Harari. The analysis of the AI trends or tendencies that will follow will stay away from presenting any such future developments as already informed by a fear of the future narrative. Stepping away from the human against machine narratives can be seen as the main rhetorical aim of my own story. The interest here is to explore the logical consequences of the developments of AI that are already taking place today. It will also take into account the dynamics of AI systems adoption by the Creative Class, which is after all the main subject of this text. Lastly, it will also do my best to bring back to the narratives about future AI the often neglected role of AI developers and designers. As AI researchers Chubb et al. (2022) rightly remind us, in the vast majority of science fiction narratives designers, programmers and even the operators are invisibilized, which allows for (sci-fi) authors to focus exclusively, in turn, on the human versus the machine narrative, which adds to the sense that going from AI to AGI is inevitable.

Possible Futures

What kind of predictions can we actually make about AI? And, with what degree of certainty?

Theorist, political advisor and first head of the European Bank for Reconstruction and Development Jacques Attali, and unapologetic technocrat, offered a detailed prediction of societies up to the year 2100 in his 2009 *A Brief History of the Future*, making the general observations that "every prediction is first and foremost a meditation on the present", and that a work of prediction is "also a political work" (Attali 2009, p. xvii). While distant from Attali's technocratic faith, my social futurology on AI does share the same starting point. The biggest challenge from the outset is that today both our grasp of AI systems and our understanding of the human intellect and creativity are limited (Manovich 2023a, p. 4). Some of these limitations have been discussed earlier and will therefore avoid moving forward under the assumption they are willy-nilly resolved by the passage of time. A parallel to this analysis can be perhaps made with the predictions made by economists with regard to a recession, an inflationary spiral or a crash in the stock market. It doesn't escape this text that economists are famously bad at predicting any of those things, despite them being the specialists on the matter.[19] Does that make economic analysis of potential scenarios or tendencies pointless? It doesn't, inasmuch as we don't conflate the direction marked by a tendency with the certainty of specific magnitudes. An economist can in the same way identify the consequences of pursuing specific actions with varied levels of specificity: for instance, the impact of a sustained decrease or increase of fiscal policy, the impact on prices of a supply shock or a long-term decrease of investment in a country's energy infrastructure. Analysing the consequences of such scenarios is not pseudoscientific or unreasonable. The argument here will remain sound, by focusing on developing the logical consequences of events already unfolding today, like, for example, the rapid adoption of AI systems within the creative industries or customer service departments. The analysis can be seen as an exploration of possible scenarios and potential unintended consequences, without claiming that multiple scenarios can't occur in parallel or that a determined path is inevitable. Furthermore, the analysis will avoid making assumptions about technological progress that have no clear link to the state of AI today; it will avoid scenarios that presume the existence of AGI. Ultimately, more attention will be given to the social, political and economic consequences of the use and rate of adoption of AI systems than to the prediction of specific developments in the field of ICT.

Trend 1: Automation, Replacement and Displacement

Chapter 2 showed some of the ways in which AI has led to job replacement and displacement. This section takes a step further, in order to understand where and to what extent this tendency will continue or even accelerate, while paying particular attention to its effects on the Creative Class. Economist David Spencer claims that a key aspect to understanding the behaviour of firms when it comes to the adoption of AI systems is the emphasis they put on consumer interests over worker interests. For him, AI systems have been used almost exclusively to "meet the interests of

[19] On this topic, Nate Silver's (2012) *The Signal and the Noise: Why So Many Predictions Fail-but Some Don't* provide a worthwhile analysis of why so many predictions fail.

consumers for more regular and cheaper services" (Spencer 2024, p. 5). Using Starbucks as an example, he notes that the coffee retailer has adopted digital scheduling software to directly reduce labour costs (p. 5). In doing so, workers lose control over when and how long they work, while customers gain at their expense: longer service hours benefit consumers, while cost reductions benefit the firm. To understand the incentives to use AI to reduce costs it makes sense to keep in mind the high taxes on labour relative to machinery or software, which has in the past been a driver of investment in technology (Tyson and Zysman 2022, p. 258). Despite it being a strong incentive, firms are not always able to quickly benefit from investments in new technologies, due to gaps or lags in the development of the organizational capabilities needed to effectively use them (Tyson and Zysman, p. 258). Gen AI presents a unique challenge in this respect. Effective prompting still requires hours of practice. Difficulties with multimodality make dealing with different types of input formats cumbersome and add a layer of difficulty in this respect. Tasks like video production, even for low-budget productions, require today for networks of creative workers to simultaneously deal with text, imagery, music and video assets. There is no direct transference of skills that, for example, allows a video editor to immediately use a text-to-video AI like Sora or Runway. Firms need to have a clear vision of what it is that they expect from these tools and how they see them incorporated into current workflows. An expectation of immediate cost reductions may not come to fruition and is likely to discourage some firms in the short term. This allows, at the same time, for creative workers who learn to use these systems on their own initiative to gain a competitive edge. Any such edge, however, may prove fleeting, if companies like OpenAI focus on reducing prompting to a one-shot process, which would all but ensure that firms who remain laggards would simply disappear. The fate of creatives who become highly proficient in the art of prompting across different Gen AI systems is difficult to foresee in this context. Moreover, in the medium and longer terms, business expectations go beyond cost reductions and are led by the hopes of increased worker productivity. Looking back at changes in productivity in the past forty years, when the personal computer, the Internet and smartphones were introduced, is a good place to start, in order to assess what firms can expect from adopting AI. Similar promises of high productivity accompanied the introduction of past technologies, and the unfortunate reality for enthusiasts is that the evidence does not seem to match the expectations: US productivity growth slowed during the second half of the twentieth century as computer technologies were introduced, and this was also true for other advanced economies (Tyson and Zysman, p. 259). The answer may again lie on the type of expectations that are raised by the true believers, such as McKinsey's claim that AI would free between 60 and 70% of workers' time. Unsurprisingly, Acemoglu and Johnson (2023) conclude that the productivity benefits of effective complementarity between workers and technologies are not currently being realized, at least not to a significant degree, for a simple reason: "human-complementary machines are not attractive to organisations when they are intent on cost cutting" (p. 332). There is, thus, an important tension between long-term productivity and short-term cost reductions that is rarely acknowledged by firms and their consultancies. There is no shortage of researchers in business and organizational science that seem to ignore the lack of fruition of past predictions, claiming, for instance, in the advertising industry, that AI systems will in the near future "streamline various processes, including ideation, research, and content generation … craft marketing materials such as social media posts, articles, and emails" (Gupta et al. 2024, p. 3).

Keeping the past in mind may still explain the anxiety that applications of AI, like AI-Art, still generate among artists and researchers. Looking back at the impact of photography, for example, McLoughlin (2024) argues, AI systems are already a threat in fields like concept art and digital design "where the product of an artist's work is rapidly becoming less distinguishable from that of the AI models" (p. 4). Zylinska (2020) shares those same concerns. Yet, following their logic leads us to the uneasy question of should photography have better not been invented then? The reality is that history shows that whether photography, computers, design software or robotics, creators have not only been able to incorporate them into their creative process, but challenge and expand the narrow uses that often bring them to life in the first place. In other words, creators have in the past been successful at learning to use, challenge and incorporate new technologies. Chapter 1 of this book discussed different examples of computational creativity to make this point clear. The real question is will most in the Creative Class be able to do so when it comes to Gen AI? It's this question that makes McLoughlin's point unavoidable. It's undeniable that past technologies, from railroads to automobiles, have had disruptive effects on people's livelihoods. They can create precarious conditions for those who are displaced and are left to fend for themselves, which can be especially bad under the meritocratic, winner-takes-all attitude of

Neoliberalism. Yet, when it comes to harmful effects on people's livelihoods, the appropriation of creative value, of intellectual property, is something perhaps more pressing and even more anxiety inducing. Gen AI can help firms increase shareholder value, not only by reducing the costs of labour, but by capturing the "general intellect" contained in their vast training datasets. Let's not forget that LLMs are trained on data that has been basically acquired for free. In the coming decade these data-hungry systems will push their owners to expand way beyond their currently available data. Intellectual property battles will take place, and relatively strong creators, established in their field and wealthy enough to take on the costs that legal processes entail, will, no doubt, fare better than up and coming creators who cannot afford these costs. In industries like advertising and marketing communications, where most of the output lives in the public domain, it's easy to see how future AI systems could be trained on the history of TV commercials, for instance, and used to create a stream of cheap, relatively high-quality video ads that even small firms can afford. Their output will no doubt be unoriginal and may even feel repetitive, but this is unlikely to discourage brands that are eager to reduce their marketing budgets. The likelihood that in such a scenario creators would be able to claim any sort of intellectual property rights is near zero. The incentives to continue hiring experienced creators, under such circumstances, will begin to dwindle. It's only by leveraging the competitive edge of early adoption that creators have a fighting chance to avoid making such initiatives worthwhile for predatory investors. Only by maintaining a noticeable creative edge over outputs that simply repeat and iterate creations from the past will there be an incentive for firms to be willing to pay a premium for human creators.

There is, however, another factor that could potentially accelerate work replacement and displacement, even while bypassing the hopes of higher productivity: the shortage of workers experienced in many developed economies. A decreasing or stalled supply of human labour sets the stage for the incorporation of AI systems, albeit less with a focus on creators and more on nurses, social workers, counsellors and psychologists, all of which demand higher levels of emotional intelligence. Japan, for example, leads the way in robot use in places where emotional engagement is core to their function, such as nursing homes and hospitals, where filling the supply of human labour available may include both replacement and complementarity (Tyson and Zysman 2022, p. 265). The main retort to this tendency is the claim that human emotions are essential to these jobs, because positive human interactions require an emotional connection that AI systems are simply unable to replicate.[20] While it's true that deep human relationships have stronger emotional content, it's wrong to assume that we live in a world where all human interactions are meant to deliver strong emotional connections. We must honestly ask ourselves, how many of the human interactions we have outside of our circle of family and friends are purely transactional? Take, for example, customer relationship management. Whether through support lines or face-to-face retail sales, it can hardly be seen as intended to generate strong bonds between customers and company employees. Such relationships are designed to be solely transactional in nature, making them precisely for this reason, apt for replacement with AI systems like chatbots, built on LLMs like ChatGPT. A more interesting question is whether firms still see value in an actors' ability to establish strong interpersonal relationships with their consumers, to the point that they are incentivized to keep certain jobs in the hands of humans or deterred from adopting and implementing AI.[21] The more market-based human interactions become overall, the more transactional they will be as a result, and the more prone to be replaceable by AI systems. Following this logic allows us to see that the replacement of human-to-human interactions for human-to-AI ones is not only plausible but very likely. While work that combines physical and emotional labour, like nursing, will still require a robotic component to any AI, it remains the case that this view is consistent with both the transactional nature of customer relationships and the strong incentives for cost-cutting that rule current corporate mindsets. Unsurprisingly, AI-to-human interactions are not confined to customer service and can be found in virtually all exchange relationships, mediated by selling and renting platforms, including job matching services (gig workers to tasks) (Tyson and Zysman, pp. 262–263). In the near future as the data on which LLMs is expanded, AI-to-human interactions may potentially include legal advice and services, accounting and tax services as well as medical diagnosis (e.g. laboratory tests, x-rays, etc.). In a very recent development, the *Harvard Business Review* reports that in 2025 the top three use cases for LLMs are Therapy and

[20] Tyson and Zysman argue in this respect that it's unlikely that they are able to replace or displace humans in "high-level cognitive demand tasks involving reasoning, real-world knowledge, judgment, and social interactions" (p. 257).

[21] Sheffi (2024) makes an interesting point on the fallibility of systems themselves, arguing that human ability to communicate and establish interpersonal connections is crucial when "systems fail and people need to overcome their difficulties by working together" (p. 349).

companionship, Organizing my life and Finding purpose (Zao-Sanders 2025). All three use cases directly relate to the emotional labour done commonly by psychologists, counsellors and life coaches. These developments likely respond to a variety of factors, including the economic costs of therapy of coaching sessions, which may simply be prohibitive for many people. At the same time, they seem to confirm Neoliberalism's transformation of human interactions into purely transactional ones. After all, one can only wonder why people would prefer to use an LLM to discuss their problems, fears and setbacks rather than doing it with their family and friends. While it's true that ChatGPT will not judge our behaviour, it's also true that it cannot empathize in any way with our life experience and the emotional pressures that people face in a hyper-individualistic society.[22]

Trend 2: Uneasy Creativity, Between Accessibility and Staleness

One of the most common arguments in favour of incorporating AI systems into creative networks is that it turns creativity from a domain of the few into a domain of the many. In other words, AI systems democratize creativity. Björn Ommer, group leader of the Machine Vision & Learning Group at LMU, argues along these lines that, "the model removes a barrier to ordinary people expressing their creativity" (Revolutionizing image generation by AI 2022). The makers of text-to-image generator Stable Diffusion agree with the sentiment, stating on their Website, that their AI system "will empower billions of people to create stunning art within seconds" (Stable Diffusion Launch Announcement 2022).

AI researchers Pieters and Winiger grant some validity to these claims too, by reminding us that technology has already in past decades served a similar role in areas like music production, graphic design and video creation. In today's world, they note, AI systems "are empowering non-experts and experts alike to be more creative, more of the time. One could say, the price of creation is falling" (Pieters and Winiger 2016). AI systems are lowering the "high barrier to entry" for those without particular skills or talents. If creative tasks can be mastered in short notice and access to AI

[22] The paper adds as well that phenomenon is not specific to the West but is equally true in China. According to the author "AI-delivered therapeutic interventions have reached a level of sophistication such that they're indistinguishable from human-written therapeutic responses" (Zao-Sanders 2025).

is more or less universal, then the term "expert" needs to be either abandoned or redefined.

There are two key aspects to the democratization of creativity argument. First an economic one, highlighting the way in which technology can lower the market entry costs of new participants. Let's take music production as an example. While in, say, the 1970s producing an album required equipment that was prohibitively expensive for most starting musicians, by the 2010s these same starting musicians would be able to record, mix, edit and master their tracks with the help of relatively inexpensive software that can run on the average laptop. The second aspect entails both economic and sociological consequences. When we say that AI systems allow people with no acquired skills and no previous experience to deliver outputs that are comparable to the outputs delivered by those with skills and experience, this implies that the labour costs of producing such outputs decrease. Yet, its implications don't stop there. If anyone is able to match the creative output of today's experts, then the social value conferred to those who are part of creative networks will decrease and perhaps disappear entirely in the long run. People's value in a Neoliberal society is certainly dictated by their incomes, but also by the perceived social benefits of what they do. When we say that teachers and nurses are worth much more than what they are paid for, this sentiment confirms that fact. If, however, anyone could be a nurse without the need to acquire skills or experience, then the perceived social benefits of people choosing to become nurses are substantially lowered. It could even reach a point where it's worth noting: if anyone from a child to an octogenarian, regardless their education, would be able to deliver the same type of care than a professional nurse with years of experience can, then it becomes irrelevant to that society whether people train and practise to become nurses. A fate of this kind could await creativity, making the begging question: how would such an event unfold and what counter forces could it encounter?

Sticking to the economic side of the argument, which emphasizes the lower costs of creative outputs, allows us to draw parallels to the disruptive role that reproduction machines played in the past, from the printing press to the photographic camera. Philosopher Walter Benjamin was preoccupied with the phenomenon of mechanical reproduction at the beginning of the twentieth century. Benjamin (2018) saw technology as debasing the value of art to the point where artworks would become commodities rather than valued objects of admiration. What would be the worth of an original Matisse, for example, if anyone could have a photography of it?

We enjoy today an availability of inexpensive reproductions of masterpieces from any era, which can be bought across a myriad of online stores. It's true nonetheless that the originals have neither lost their value nor people see them as equivalent to their reproductions. Is this simply explained by an irrational appreciation of the original? Perhaps to some extent, yet Benjamin's argument on reproduction is unsuitable, because reducing AI-based outputs and digital media in general to a contemporary form of reproduction, to a printing press 2.0, misses much of the point about the importance of experimentation with a new medium: " 'Reproduction' is to the digital world what the hot-air balloon once was to aviation. Using digital technology artists are now able to introduce new forms of 'production' not 'reproduction' " (Rush 2005, p. 181). Whether using graphic design software, music mixing and editing software, all the way to creating robots like Moura's artbots, the creative use of technology persists, because creators have been able to rethink these technologies, beyond their capacity for reproduction. Could this not happen as well with AI systems? It could, yet the patent risk of this supposed democratization of creativity is that by allowing anyone, regardless of skill and experience, to fulfil creative tasks with the help of AI, it sets us on a path of stagnation and repetition. Let's bring back to mind the fact that LLMs are always trained on an existing pool of data; they may even be trained on all the artworks and cultural artefacts that have existed. Their output, notwithstanding, is constrained to a finite data space, and even if the set of outputs possible is mathematically vast, it will never stop being self-referential, which is why Manovich (2023a) referred to AI as a very conservative artist (p. 2). As researchers Zhou and Lee (2024) argue, this is highly problematic because "[w]ithout establishing new frontiers for creative exploration, AI systems trained on outdated knowledge banks run the risk of perpetuating the generation of generic content at a mass scale in a self-reinforcing cycle" (p. 6). Moreover, the consequences of this purported democratization of creativity are far from being a vision about a distant future. Its odd consequences have already earned it a place in popular culture, which named this phenomenon of omnipresent AI content as *slop*.

The term AI slop defines both the quality and the quantity of AI-generated content of all types that is flooding the Internet through social accounts, tabloids and blog sites: "It's not disinformation. It's vague text, filled with buzzwords, with no real point. It's a hastily made meme illustration of a celebrity or a politician. It's a news article where something about the tone or the facts doesn't seem right" (Adami 2024). The idea resembles past expressions, like "pink slime", referring to vast amounts of poor-quality online content that is often politically motivated. Despite the apparent difference of each of these articles or images, there is a recognizable style to them, which is the direct result of the AI systems' default aesthetic choices. A major issue with much of AI-based art today is that it often creates differences without purpose. While outcomes can't always be predicted, they frequently lack significance. The consequences are often muddled by the apparent simplicity of using Gen AI and by the arguments of democratization. In actuality, as Zylinska (2020) puts it, "much of current AI art, especially of the computer-and data-based kind, ends up generating an odd combination of the fuzzy, the mindless and the bland" (p. 73).

Slop is illustrative of how regardless of subject matter, approach or artistic intention, if all creative outputs are the result of a single process, sameness is built into the system. What process? An algorithmically mediated process that defines a canon of aesthetic and thematic standards. This is not dissimilar to the role of the nineteenth-century art salons. These salons grew greatly in popularity, yet so did the sense that they encouraged a formulaic and normative view of art that soon felt outmoded. While creativity didn't disappear, it became clear for the creators of the time, creators like Monet, Renoir and Cezanne, that "truly creative work had to be done outside it and in pointed opposition to the system of art-theoretical values it embodied" (McLoughlin 2024, p. 9). We may look at slop and simply dismiss it as a pastiche that can't possibly be expected to have the authority of the nineteenth-century salon. What gives slop a real potential to shape how we understand creativity is, both, its ubiquitous nature and the low effort and low production costs that it requires. Slop is not confined to a few strange places in the vast sea of the Internet. It's on the contrary a tsunami that threatens to flood every corner of it, because no creative network can ever match the volumes of slop produced on a daily basis. If we consider that Gen AI is still in its infancy, in terms of adoption, it's easy to see that what already feels like a tsunami could in the near future be seen as the first driblets of water flowing through a widening dam crack. Although, why wouldn't most people just reject or ignore the slop? As media theorist Marcel Marburger (2024) explains, a big factor driving the popularity of AI-generated content is the simple fact that the artworld and the creative industries more broadly are today "full of works whose creative potential is also inadequate" (p. 5). In a world driven primarily by firms that insist on cost-cutting and short-term profits, AI slop may seem like manna falling from heaven to many CEOs in the creative industries.

A scenario of ever-present slop may begin with a growing sense of staleness but leads towards the shaping and regulating of tastes and creative markets.[23] In the process, the social value of creative networks is diminished and ultimately leads to the banalization of creativity, a future where the term basically becomes meaningless and archaic. A world where AI-generated creativity becomes the norm is, in turn, one where the process of deterritorialization-territorialization that animates the most interesting forms of computational creativity is no longer possible. As Zylinska (2020) puts it, "Dreamy neural network art of this kind thus ultimately has a pacifying effect, anaesthetising us into the perception of banal sameness that creates an illusion of diversification without being able to account for differences that matter" (p. 83).[24]

What would await the Creative Class in this scenario? The social consequences of creative stagnation would be for those in the creative economy a reduction of their work to what the late David Graeber called a "Bullshit job":

> In a truly bullshit job, it's often entirely unclear what one is really supposed to be doing, what one can say about what one is and isn't doing, who one can ask and what one can ask them, how much and within what parameters one is expected to pretend to be working, and what sorts of things it is or is not permissible to do instead. This is a miserable situation. The effects on

[23] Zylinska sees AI as a new form of agency that facilitates such outcomes. She argues, "AI is here more than just a tool: it becomes an active agent in shaping tastes, regulating markets and defining what counts as mainstream visuality. The work of art is therefore not just mechanically reproduced but also algorithmically produced" (Zylinska 2020, p. 69).

[24] She calls this state of affairs neurototalitarianisms, defined as "the utter intensification of semiotic (but we may also add, visual) simulation, in the end resulting in the sensation of panic in the social—and individual—neuro-system. 'in this condition of panic, reason becomes unable to master the flow of events or to process the semio-stimulations released into the infosphere'. Would it be a step too far to state that AI-art can actually be mobilised, wittingly or unwittingly, in the service of neurototalitarianism, using cutesy kittens and spaghetti with eyes to capture not just the attention but also the cognitive and neurological sphere of the modern political subject? This form of art enforces what Berardi has described as 'mental subsumption', whereby the automation of vision and of cognitive activity paves the way for the emergence of constantly stimulated yet passive subjectivity" (Zylinska, p. 83).

> health and self-esteem are often devastating. Creativity and imagination crumble. (Graeber 2018, p. 199)

Furthermore, Graeber's words on the dashed hopes that resulted from seeing the Internet go from a space of freedom and knowledge to a gated platform world of social media sameness remain relevant to a future of ubiquitous AI slop:

> [T]he situation has sparked an efflorescence of social media (Facebook, YouTube, Instagram, Twitter): basically, of forms of electronic media that lend themselves to being produced and consumed while pretending to do something else. I am convinced this is the primary reason for the rise of social media, especially when one considers it in the light not just of the rise of bullshit jobs but also of the increasing bullshitization of real jobs. (Graeber 2018, p. 201)

Does this all mean that we should advocate for restrictions or full bans on Gen AI? This seems to me entirely unrealistic, leaving us however with only one serious way out. Participants of the Creative Class in particular must remain highly sceptical and critical of those who advocate for the so-called democratization of creativity, by showing that their advocacy is either naive or self-serving, running counter to the interests of the Creative Class. More broadly, countering stagnation means encouraging creative networks to redefine the use of Gen AI, highlighting the need for experimentation. This means, specifically, using their proprietary data to train AI systems in a way that modifies their default responses. It also means having the ability to update and retrain models on a regular basis, in order to produce fundamental differences on the type of patterns and styles that determine their outputs.

Trend 3: Collaboration and Complementarity

The text has so far focused on potentially harmful scenarios, where the universal adoption of Gen AI leads to the stagnation of creativity and the precarization of the Creative Class. The last section ended, nonetheless, by returning to the idea of experimentation, which has been fundamental in the history of computation creativity and the history of art in general. This connects too, with the idea of augmented creativity presented in Chap. 2 of this text. This section will, therefore, explore a path where augmented creativity can become a reality in the near future. It will focus on the conditions needed to transform this scenario into a real future for the Creative Class, including a better understanding of the limitations of LLMs, from the perspective of collaboration.

In order to take control of the future we must begin with a clear vision that ensures AI systems will be a positive addition to creative networks, in whichever industry they may operate. Pieters and Winiger (2016) propose a vision to design systems that can negotiate the creative process, augment our overall creative capabilities and accelerate the skill acquisition time, from novice to expert. A prerequisite for this vision is for creative networks and firms to step away from reducing creativity to individual talent. Creativity, it's been argued, is networked through and through, and the role of experienced, talented individuals is to lead and forge a culture of innovation and experimentation that focuses on challenging old ideas, in order to deliver relevant novelty. A successful adoption of AI systems is hence not measured by how many individuals are able to use and deliver AI-generated content. Such a route shapes AI adoption by the Creative Class as a cut-throat competition against peers that hinders rather than facilitates the transfer of knowledge. We must also acknowledge rather than obfuscate the fact that the value of AI systems does not reside in its algorithms or its compute, but in the quality of the data it is trained on. This data is a social good; it's created by millions of humans across a variety of industries and scientific domains. Just like a social media platform derives its value from the content generated by its users, so does AI derive its value from its data. Outdated, biased and poor-quality data render AI systems useless, no matter how advanced their internal architecture may be. Enabling a future of collaboration, therefore, begins with an effort from its users to improve the quality of the training data. It begins too with a better understanding of neural networks and the overall inner workings of the system. A vision conducive to augmented creativity will require for all actors involved, not just developers, to have a better understanding of AI systems. In other words, making the medium visible is fundamental to a future where AI systems complement rather than replace the actors within a creative network. Understanding how these AI systems operate goes beyond proficiency in the mathematics of multidimensional spaces and generative algorithms. It's mainly about understanding the weaknesses and strengths of these systems, so we can better define what their role within a creative network should be.[25] Only at this point will an experimental mindset come into play. It will be needed to ensure that the role of AI systems is not to fulfil tasks but to provide new perspectives, to allow creators to see the world in ways that are humanly impossible or to envision new worlds entirely. Reducing the role of AI to fulfilling tasks would mean, on the contrary, defining human-AI interaction as little more than a game of getting factual answers to factual questions. We can think of this as using a text-to-image generator exclusively to provide realistic representations of the world. This route is unfortunately gaining traction fast and it's a common one in advertising, where the only driver seems to be cost-savings, meaning savings when conducting a shoot, buying a copyrighted photograph or creating copy for an ad. This approach completely ignores the fact that photographers interpret the world through their lens and that no medium, including their camera, is simply neutral; once again, the medium is the message.[26] Every image used is already an interpretation of the world, and the text has shown that AI systems' default interpretation is biased as well as censorious, omitting certain depictions as politically incorrect or offensive. The daily frustration that many early adopters have with AI systems that generate human depictions that seem imperfect, overly polished and soulless is a manifestation of the logic of task fulfilment at work.[27] The answer to this logic is, to restate, to use AI systems as a medium for experimentation. In the words of Brian Eno (2020), "Whatever you find weird, ugly, uncomfortable and nasty about a new medium will surely become its signature [...] so much modern art is the sound of things going out of control, of a medium pushing to its limits and breaking apart. Being creative means departing from the established path. The problem-solving logic that transforms AI systems into black boxes sets the Creative Class for failure, because it doesn't just define the role of AI as a task-fulfilling tool but also has the unintended consequence of narrowing down all creativity to predefined tasks. The fact that very

[25] Pease and Colton (2011) similarly argue, "Humans and machines have different strengths, and instead of trying to squeeze machines into a way of thinking that is human, we should aim to develop computer systems that make the most of their power" (p. 4).

[26] As Aydin (2022) argues, "the view of technologies not being neutral has been defended from a range of perspectives.

[27] McCormack et al. (2023) confirm this fact, claiming that "it is common for AI artists to try and hide or fix errors generated by TTI systems. But exploiting these limitations might lead to more interesting artistic possibilities" (p. 14).

little is being done, outside of the artworld proper, to challenge this logic reveals that, in a strange way, AI ultimately shows that humans too often behave like machines themselves.[28] Still, it's fair to ask whether the limitations of Gen AI to produce novelty outside of its data space not represent an insurmountable barrier for creators. It's true that Gen AI's training limits a neural network's ability to push boundaries and break paradigms, yet their strength lies in their ability to see patterns that we cannot. Artist and technologist Refik Anadol shows how such experiments can deliver completely unexpected outcomes. In his work *Unsupervised,* Anadol trains an AI system on MOMA's two hundred years of modern art collection (MOMA 2022). The AI system is then used to reimagine this history. The result is a visually staggering work that reinterprets the history of styles and colours that unfolds in real time. What the public encounters is a mix of fantasy and hallucinations that challenge any rational interpretation of that same history, revealing unexpected iterations of colours and themes. The AI system's training includes elements from the environment, such as sound, changes in light and movement that provide a layer of uniqueness to the event. A somewhat similar example comes from AI researchers Lisi et al. (2020), who demonstrated that it's feasible to anticipate the evolution of styles in visual art by training an AI system to identify certain evolutionary patterns through the analysis of extensive image databases. The AI system made predictions that closely align with the actual historical evolution of art styles, which highlights the "algorithmic" nature of many stylistic developments. This suggested that these developments might not solely result from historical events or unique artistic innovations but can be instead seen as the inevitable result of inherent formal principles. Furthermore, the system could also forecast upcoming art styles, using predictions that, while not necessarily predetermined, stemmed from a limited set of combinations. Those purported future developments are, therefore, a product of a range of finite combinations that data analysis systems can detect and reproduce, but humans cannot (Arielli and Manovich 2022, p. 11). Both examples show how AI systems can be used to see things in large volumes of data that humans are unable to, but it

[28] Zylinska (2020) makes a similar point when saying that "being creative means diverging from the established path we carve out and then follow each day" and concludes following Satoy that "machines might ultimately help us, as humans, to behave less like machines" (p. 66).

does more than that. It challenges the humanist paradigm, by showing that what we often perceive as the product of subjective and incommensurable human experiences can actually follow a path of development that is not completely unpredictable. It shows that we act like machines more than we allow ourselves to believe. Potential collaborations with AI should start, therefore, by using AI to disclose our own limitations and our own biases.

In this sense, another important challenge on our collaboration path with AI is the shortcomings of prompting as the main means for interaction. Prompts are not merely commands, but in a way are also interpretations, mediated through language, that the creator hopes the AI system is able to bring to life through its generated outputs. Language is perhaps the medium that most often feels invisible, due to the seemingly natural role that it plays in our social life. As a medium, language commonly simplifies a range of emotions and intentions whose meaning can get lost or be misinterpreted by others. The popular phrase "getting lost in translation" perfectly captures the experience that we all have, when the language we use fails to truly capture what we want to say or to fully translate what others do. The twentieth century saw many debates on the nature of language. Intellectual figures like Wittgenstein, Austin, Searle, Derrida and Chomsky contributed enormously to this debate, and it would go far beyond the scope of this text to provide a close examination of their ideas and disagreements. Suffice it to say here, language can't be reduced to descriptions of objects or actions, which, in turn, means that using language exclusively for that fails to grasp its real function in social life. How does this impact our interaction with AI systems? Artist and researcher John McCormack outlines the problem neatly: test-to-image systems that use a literal understanding of an image "produce images which are themselves comprehensible in that language. Extraneous 'meaning, intention or encoded information assigned to a specific textual construct, be it metaphorical or culturally charged, will be lost in translation' " (McLoughlin 2024, p. 4).[29] We only need to think of works of art like Picasso's *Guernica*

[29] AI developers and researchers already contend with the issue of language polysemy, words carrying different meanings depending on their context. In neural networks matching concepts to specific neurons is a desirable but so far unattainable characteristic. "Although some strides have been made in visualizing the contributions of individuals nodes in complex networks, most observers would acknowledge that neural networks as a whole remain something of a black box" (Marcus 2018, p. 11).

or Van Gogh's *Starry Night* to quickly grasp the limitations we face when trying to capture their meaning and value through words alone.

Gen AI systems like Midjourney categorize images based on descriptions that attempt to capture their visual identity through simple combinations: "a teddy bear on a table", "a pink flower in a vase", etc. This categorization limits the system's use of language to literal translations that ignores commonly used literary devices like metaphors, allegories or colloquialisms, as well as cultural expressions and even memes. Moreover, text-to-image generators struggle too with "producing diagrammatic or abstract images, where lines, annotations, dimensions, shading colour and texture are loaded with information beyond their mere graphic expression" (McLoughlin, p. 4). The role of creators is, to be sure, essential to push the boundaries of prompting, helping AI developers, trapped in a domain that fixates on a descriptive use language, consider its non-literal nature, especially when it comes to rethinking its impact on creative outputs.

Given these hurdles, how can it be argued that Gen AI has real potential to augment creativity?

McCormack et al. (2023) conclude, for instance, that AI-art in its current form has a parasitic relationship with human creativity, where one benefits at the expense of the other, actively harming human artists. While in line with McCormack's concerns, this text has also discussed examples from artists that have been able to use AI systems in novel ways. Researchers Zhou and Lee (2024) analyse the impact of AI adoption by creators, assessing both the impact on their specific work and their perception of the impact on creativity as a whole.[30] Perhaps surprisingly, they conclude that creators who excel at producing new ideas, prior to the adoption of AI, produce work that is most favourably evaluated, once they incorporate AI. Their work shows that experience matters, because the "ability to manipulate novel concepts and curate artworks based on coherence are relevant skills when using text-to-image AI" (Zhou and Lee, p. 6). They add that their conclusions are not based solely on a creator's technical proficiency, but on ideation proficiency and the ability to think of their work contextually. The adoption of Gen AI, they argue, should move

[30] Their research focuses on three questions: (1) how does the adoption of Generative AI affect humans' creative production?, (2) is Generative AI enabling humans to produce more creative content? and (3) when and for whom does the adoption of Generative AI lead to more creative and valuable artefacts?

forward under the idea of generative synesthesia, defined as a "human–AI co creative process [...] in which AI-assisted artistic creation is driven by ideas and filtering [allowing for] the harmonization of human exploration and AI exploitation to discover new creative workflows" (Zhou and Lee, p. 7). This means, regarding the question of whether AI can be creative, that the definitive answer is and should remain that AI can only be creative, when it becomes part of a process of collaboration and co-creation that is led by human creators.[31] This process of collaboration shouldn't be seen as a static methodology, but as a dynamic adaptive process that ensures human-AI co-creation leads to qualitative differences.[32] This includes the introduction of randomness, intent and the consecution of a work-public encounter that fosters active and not only passive consumption of images.[33]

So, what is the best way to get to this future of AI-human collaboration? Following sociologist Richard Sennett, we must keep in mind that across time and culture rituals have been the best way to maintain group cohesion, because they "relieve and resolve anxiety, by turning people outward in shared, symbolic acts" (Sennet 2012, p. 293). Rituals can play a strong role in changing the narrative around creativity from a focus on talented individuals to a focus on creative networks, from a focus on problem solving to a focus on experimentation. Rituals reinforce values and cooperation, helping emphasize the type of orientation that certain activities, like creative work, within particular groupings, like creative networks,

[31] Along these lines my proposal agrees with Moruzzi (2023), who claims "artificial systems should be regarded as co-creative partners for humans, not as mere tools or as isolated agents" (p. 261). In greater depth I would ascribe to Manovich (2024) when he states "I want an AI that does not make any art on its own. Instead, this AI would use algorithms to analyze an artist's works and provide them with insights and new ideas. It could visualize changing patterns in the artworks made over time in subject and form and suggest possible directions for experiments. It could identify which techniques the artist employs frequently and infrequently and encourage the use of more uncommon ones. In other words, even though such AI wouldn't automate the creation of art (and why would we want this anyway?), it could offer artists something more valuable: intelligent feedback and even dialogue".

[32] McLoughlin (2024) argues similarly that "the creation of AI-based works of art leads us to conclude that both parties, the human and the technological, are engaged in the creation process. The participation of human and technological actors changes the situation and both actors. This is known as the co-shaping process between humans and technologies (p. 7)".

[33] Terzidis et al. (2023) phrase it as unintentional intentionality, arguing "A work of art will be judged 'artistic' to the extent that humans will recognize an artistic intent in the work itself. In particular, the introduction of random processes makes an AI-generated artwork fully independent of human creativity" (Terzidis et al., p. 1715).

should have for their social value to persist. Under this lens, the development of skills and expertise, for example, is better seen as a type of a ritual, where rhythm blends meaning and practice (Sennet 2012, p. 215). As argued in Chap. 1, such an approach can be seen as a constant negotiation between creators and materials, and a discussion about the place that each actor occupies within a particular network. A ritualistic view of creativity also means that any authority ascribed to a creator will come from their skill as much as from their ability to mentor; obedience is in this context a signal that the mentee is ready to embark on a journey towards mastering a craft (Sennett 2008, p. 54). Sennett underscores the importance of dedication and focus that is both reinforced through rituals and is necessary to achieve true expertise (p. 20). His point couldn't be timelier, when we consider that in 2023 only 33% of US workers said to be engaged at work and that engagement has hovered around 30% since the 2000 (Harter 2024). If AI systems are going to re-engage rather than alienate the Creative Class, then the role of rituals to stress the importance of perfecting a craft cannot be underestimated. A good craftsman, he argues, "chooses the machine, not so much because of its mechanical or functional capabilities, but because it reveals something about the nature of her craft" (Sennett 2008, p.106). The good craftsman is not in awe of machines and, hence, doesn't incorporate a machine into their work because of their functional capabilities alone, but because "it reveals something about the nature of her craft" (p. 106). Like good craftsmen, creators don't simply operate machines, but "propose rather than command [...] thus, their uses are fashioned with complete acknowledgement, but without fear, about the operator's own limitations" (p. 105). What Sennett refers to as fear is the fear of failure that strangles experimentation and we know by now that meritocracy can spark that fear, by making failure a punishable offence. Furthermore, getting away from the traps of fear of failure and embracing experimentation will require the relationship between creative networks across industries, including the art industry and academic research, to intensify and grow deeper than what it is today. The argument here would agree with Luitse and Denkena (2021) when they claim that "critical scholarship [...] is crucial to advancing the development of techniques and systems that provide alternative ways of 'doing AI' and therefore contribute to different understandings about AI's possibilities and applications, out of reach from the confining embrace of big tech companies" (p. 11).

As stated earlier, such an attitude of experimentation requires that AI systems, currently trained exclusively on opaque pre-training data, be opened up, so users can add their own data into the system as well. The creative work of Lev Pereulkov is exemplary in this respect. Pereulkov fine-tuned the text-to-image system Stable Diffusion (model 2.1) using his own dataset, composed of forty paintings by well-known Russian conceptual artists, including Erik Bulatov, Ilya Kobakov, Irina Nakhova, among others. He created a series of images titled *artificial experiments 1–10*, using his customized data to show defining stylistic features of their work, but also the surreal and absurd semantics that characterize their work (Manovich 2023b, p. 3). In other words, Pereulkov shows how a predefined AI system can deliver completely different and unexpected results through the introduction of a relatively small set of new data. A future where collaboration and augmented creativity become synonymous with terms like AI-Art is possible. The intensive experimentation by creators like Trevor Plagem, Lev Manovich and Refik Anadol is already showing us how to transform these systems into much more than tools, and surely much more than task fulfillers. Whether this scenario will come to fruition is not guaranteed, in the same way as a scenario of banalization and staleness is not predetermined either. Strong headwinds await either path. The role of powerful economic actors, driven by short-term interests, cannot be underestimated and will have to be openly resisted. Taking distance from an individualistic view on creativity is a necessary starting point. Beyond that, the most effective form of resistance comes down to the ability of creators of all industries to use AI systems in ways that challenge the domesticated expectations of corporate heads and investors. The idea that creativity is but a task to be fulfilled must be rejected. Emphasizing the role of relevant novelty within creative networks is the only real leverage that the Creative Class possesses. Simply put, once the experimentation genie is out of the bottle, it will hopefully be impossible to get it back inside. This would make augmented creativity the only realistic avenue for firms powered by the Creative Class to travel.

Conclusion: What AI Tells Us About Ourselves

> The creative age requires nothing short of a change of worldview… We must begin to think of creativity as a common good, like liberty or security. It's something essential that belongs to all of us, and that must always be

nourished, renewed, and maintained—or else it will slip away. Richard Florida, *The Flight of the Creative Class*

What would it take for AI to become a true partner? And can it ever become one?

Throughout this text it's been argued that creativity is networked, departing in this way from definitions of creativity that reduce it to an individual skill. Doing so expanded the term, allowing for, among others, computational creativity to be properly grasped as a highly relevant instance of creativity and explained Florida's Creative Class as a consistent definition that gathers a variety of activities, from filmmaking to game design. It allowed me to rekindle the issue of AI as a question about the role that AI played within a network rather than a question of whether AI could now or in the future possess this or that specific talent. One can conclude, in turn, that the notion of augmented creativity best captures the most ideal scenario for human creators to effectively incorporate AI into their networks, while avoiding job displacement and replacement. This too meant that in order to effectively incorporate AI, reducing AI systems to mere tools should be avoided. The question of agency was raised, not only about AI, but also about the way in which we often define human agency in absolute terms, thinking of our freedom as based on absolute autonomy or absolute novelty. Chapter 1 showed how networks redefine agency, making it relational in nature, where our ability to think and act depends entirely on our role within a network rather than on sheer will. Given that roles within a network can change, from intermediaries to mediators, using networks as a theoretical underpinning also opens the door for our own sense of self and identity to become dynamic instead of static. Networks, hence, allow us to think of agency in more pragmatic terms, and to conceive it as a dynamic reality, as one that can be in constant flux. Deleuze and Guattari use the term *becoming* to define human subjectivity, which includes our ability to create an identity for ourselves and our capacity for self-creation. Self-creation, self-development, determines our ability to shape who we are and rediscover our potential, and it may be as important for AI systems as it is for humans. Making AI into a true creative partner is not simply a question of having the right mindset. Rethinking AI's agency as a becoming is equally important, if we are to think of future and more advanced AI as a creative partner. For any form of collaboration with AI to emerge we must drop the idea of infallibility that accompanies today's talk about the future of AI. Whether in the utopian form of *Star Trek* or the dystopian form of the Hal 9000 we often assume that an advanced form of AI is not simply smarter or more capable than a human, but that it is virtually infallible—a perfect calculation machine, even if the data used in those calculations is wrong. This is why, unsurprisingly, our narratives about artificial intelligence are laced with ideological baggage, from dataism (van Dijck 2014) to surveillance capitalism (Zuboff 2019) and all sorts of mathematical idealizations (Watson 2019), which are the perfect recipe for dystopian stories, but also for a pathway of replacement and displacement to be seen as inevitable. Current thinking about "true or authentic" AGI as a perfect calculation machine hinders us from envisioning an AI system that can be a true partner for creativity. Stepping away from such an ingrained image of AGI begins by granting AI the same ability for self-development that we grant ourselves. This means thinking of AI as a continuous work in progress, where such "work" is not merely defined by technological advances in computer and semiconductor technology, but on its ability to change and to adapt to a variety of roles within a potentially vast number of networks. In this sense, we would ideally have a future where we don't talk about AGI as a godlike entity but of AIs as a myriad of collaborators with a defined space of action. The claim being made here is, however, not the same as the often-used difference between narrow AI and general AI (AGI), where the former is only capable of performing a narrow set of tasks, while the latter is able to do them all and better than a human would. Creators are not narrow human intelligences, and to be a creator you need much more than mastery of specific techniques. Creators become fully engaged with their work using their entire human capacities, including their ability to understand and respond to a historical context. In a similar way there is no reason to think about future AI systems as failures, unless they are godlike. The prejudice that progress in the field will be necessarily judged based on whether it delivers an all-powerful AGI is ideological in nature and extremely dangerous in practice. It remains too close to the transhumanist fantasies about future humans being all powerful and immortal. Both are nothing but current expressions of the same totalitarian fantasies that plague humans since the dawn of time.

Contrary to these fantasies that make ever-greater control over humans and objects alike desirable, we must rediscover the importance of indeterminacy. Indeterminacy is what allows individuals to live in constant becoming and to challenge attempts to be constrained by narrow and unchanging identities, which are usually at the service of systems that existed before us. In the same way as we have been able to rethink and redefine what terms like worker, teacher, fatherhood or motherhood mean we must also liberate AI from the burden of AGI, so it can lead to the type of future that is desirable and attainable.[34] Researchers Beerends and Ayden see in this same indeterminacy an important and constitutive aspect of the concept of intelligence itself, which informs much of current literature about AI. Keeping intelligence as an open concept rather than a narrowly defined one matters in their view, because while aspects like intuition or real-life randomness matter "intelligence is not determined by such traits. [...] intelligence cannot and should not be captured in a demarcated definition; the openness and fluidity of these concepts are not a weakness, but rather a condition for being human" (Beerends and Aydin 2024, p. 10). As Nietzsche argued, humans are "still the undetermined animal", meaning we are constantly negotiating what it means to be human, and so we must likewise negotiate our vision for AI and what its future should be (Nietzsche 2002, p. 56).

We must equally reject a purely transactional vision of creativity that sees it as a predefined set of tasks that are at most aesthetically pleasing, but which an AI system should be able to fulfil faster and cheaper than any human can. Liberating AI from its determinist and Godlike image means ultimately liberating it from a politics of centralized control, especially from a project of control at the hands of a very small group of corporations and its shareholders. Only in this way can we do justice to what creativity is, to how it comes about and avoid the staleness and eeriness of a digital world full of slop. Only in this way can we move away from seeing the creative role of AI as one of competition against humans and embrace augmented creativity as a shared political project that will help us rethink our relation to AI and to ourselves.

[34] Beerends and Aydin (2024) argue in a similar way, claiming that "an essentialist approach to the human involves de-historicizing "human nature", making it context-independent and abstracting it on the basis of a particular identification, such as rationality or empathy. The main argument we will develop is that this process of indirectly defining and essentializing humans results in an undesirable elimination of the space for humans to be indeterminate, that is, block humans' potential to be or become something else" (p. 2).

References

Acemoglu, D., & Johnson, S. 2023. *Power and progress: Our thousand-year struggle over technology and prosperity*. Hachette.

Adami, M. 2024. AI-generated slop is quietly conquering the internet. Is it a threat to journalism or a problem that will fix itself? *Reuters Institute*, November 26. https://reutersinstitute.politics.ox.ac.uk/news/ai-generated-slop-quietly-conquering-internet-it-threat-journalism-or-problem-will-fix-itself.

Arielli, E., and L. Manovich. 2022. AI-aesthetics and the anthropocentric myth of creativity. *Philpapers.org*: 1–16.

Attali, J. 2009. *A brief history of the future*. Allen & Unwin.

Aydin, C. 2022. The technological uncanny as a permanent dimension of selfhood. Technology. In *The Oxford handbook of philosophy of technology*, ed. S. Vallor, 1–21.

Beerends, S., and C. Aydin. 2024. Negotiating the authenticity of AI: How the discourse on AI rejects human indeterminacy. *AI & Society*: 1–14.

Benjamin, W. 2018 [1935]. The work of art in the age of mechanical reproduction. In *A museum studies approach to heritage*, 226–243. Routledge.

Chubb, J., D. Reed, and P. Cowling. 2022. Expert views about missing AI narratives: Is there an AI story crisis? *AI & Society*: 1107–1126.

Craig, C. 2021. The AI-copyright challenge: Tech-neutrality, authorship, and public interest. In *Osgood legal studies research paper*. Osgood Hall Law School, New York University.

Crawford, K., and T. Paglen. 2019. *Excavating AI: The politics of training sets for machine learning*, September 19. https://excavating.ai. Accessed 25 Feb 2025.

D'Amato, K. 2024. ChatGPT: Towards AI subjectivity. *AI & Society*: 1–15.

Emsley, R. 2023. ChatGPT: These are not hallucinations–they're fabrications and falsifications. *Schizophrenia* 9 (1): 1–2.

Eno, B. 2020. *A year with swollen appendices: Brian Eno's Diary*. Faber & Faber.

Farhoomand, A. F., and D. H. Druiy. 2002. Managerial information overload. *Communications of the ACM* 45 (10): 127–131.

Feng, T., et al. 2024. How far are we from AGI: Are LLMs all we need? *Transactions on Machine Learning Research*, October, arXiv preprint, arXiv:2405.10313: 1–114.

Foucault, M. 2004. *Abnormal: Lectures at the Collège de France 1974–1975*. Picador.

Graeber, D. 2018. *Bullshit jobs: A theory*. Simon & Schuster.

Grassie, W. 2011. Millennialism at the singularity: Reflections on the limits of Ray Kurzweil's exponential logic. In *Transhumanism and its critics*, ed. Gregory R. Hansell and William Grassie, 249–269. Metanexus Institute.

Gupta, R., et al. 2024. Adoption and impacts of generative artificial intelligence: Theoretical underpinnings and research agenda. *International Journal of Information Management Data Insights* 4 (1): 100232.

Harari, Y. N. 2017. *Homo Deus: A brief history of tomorrow*. HarperCollins.

Harter, J. 2024. In new workplace, U.S. employee engagement stagnates. *Gallup*, January 23. https://www.gallup.com/workplace/391922/employee-engagement-slump-continues.aspx.

IBM. 2024. *What are AI hallucinations?* https://www.ibm.com/topics/ai-hallucinations. Access 25 Feb 2025.

Kurzweil, R. 2005. *The singularity is near: When humans transcend biology*. Penguin.

Lempert, D. 2014. What is development? What is progress? The social science and humanities of utopia and futurology. *Journal of Developing Societies* 30 (2): 223–241.

Lisi, E., et al. 2020. Modelling and forecasting art movements with CGANs. *Royal Society Open Science* 7 (4): 191569.

Luitse, D., and W. Denkena. 2021. The great transformer: Examining the role of large language models in the political economy of AI. *Big Data & Society* 8 (2): 20539517211047734.

Manovich, L. 2023a. Seven arguments about AI images and generative media. Artificial aesthetics: A critical guide to AI, media and design. *Artificial Aesthetics Chapter 5*. https://manovich.net/index.php/projects/artificial-aesthetics. Accessed 25 Feb 2025.

Manovich, L. 2023b. The AI brain in the cultural archive. *Museum of Modern Art Magazine*: 2.

Manovich. 2024. Towards 'General Artistic Intelligence'? https://www.artbasel.com/stories/lev-manovich. Accessed 10 January 2025.

Marburger, M.R. 2024. Artistic intelligence vs. artificial intelligence. *Artnodes* (34): 1–7.

Marcus, G. 2018. Deep learning: A critical appraisal. arXiv preprint. arXiv:1801.00631: 1–27.

Marinetti, F. T. 2009 [1909]. The futurist manifesto. https://www.societyforasianart.org/sites/default/files/manifesto_futurista.pdf. Accessed 1 Jan 2025.

McCormack, J., et al. 2023. Is writing prompts really making art? [Conference session]. In *International conference on computational intelligence in music, sound, art and design (part of EvoStar)*, 196–211. Springer Nature.

McLoughlin, J. 2024. The work of art in the age of artificial intelligibility. *AI & Society*: 1–13.

Misra, S., and D. Stokols. 2012. Psychological and health outcomes of perceived information overload. *Environment and Behavior* 44 (6): 737–759.

MOMA. 2022. Refik Anadol unsupervised. https://www.moma.org/calendar/exhibitions/5535 Access 30 Dec 2024.

Moore, G. E. 1998 [1965]. Cramming more components onto integrated circuits. *Proceedings of the IEEE 86* (1): 82–85.

Moruzzi, C. 2023. Creative agents: Rethinking agency and creativity in human and artificial systems. *Journal of Aesthetics and Phenomenology* 9:245–268. https://doi.org/10.1080/20539320.2022.2150470.

Murray, M. 2023. Generative and AI authored artworks and copyright law. *Hastings Communications and Entertainment Law Journal* 45 (1): 26–44. https://papers.ssrn.com/sol3/papers.cfm?abstract_id=4152484.

Nietzsche, F. 2002. In *Beyond good and evil*, ed. I Horstmann RP and J. Norman. Cambridge University Press.

OpenAI. 2018. *OpenAI charter*. https://openai.com/charter. Accessed 20 Oct 2023.

Pasquinelli, M. 2023. *The eye of the master: A social history of artificial intelligence*. Verso Books.

Pasquinelli, M., and V. Joler. 2021. The Nooscope manifested: AI as instrument of knowledge extractivism. *AI & Society* 36:1263–1280. https://doi.org/10.1007/s00146-020-01097-6.

Pease, A., and S. Colton. 2011. On impact and evaluation in computational creativity: A discussion of the Turing test and an alternative proposal. In *Proceedings of the AISB symposium on AI and Philosophy*, vol. 39.

Pieters, R., and S. Winiger. 2016. Creative AI: On the democratisation & escalation of creativity. https://medium.com/@creativeai/creativeai-9d4b2346faf3. Accessed 25 Feb 2025.

Potts, J. 2018. Futurism, futurology, future shock, climate change: Visions of the future from 1909 to the present. *Journal of Multidisciplinary International Studies* 15 (1–2): 99–116.

Revolutionizing image generation by AI: Turning text into images. 2022. LMU, September 1. https://www.lmu.de/en/newsroom/news-overview/news/revolutionizing-image-generation-by-ai-turning-text-into-images.html. Accessed 1 Jan 2024.

Rush, M. 2005. *New media in art*. Thames & Hudson.

Sandel, M. 2004. The case against perfection. *The Atlantic*, April. https://www.theatlantic.com/magazine/archive/2004/04/the-case-against-perfection/302927/.

Sennet, R. 2012. *Together: The rituals, pleasures and politics of cooperation*. Yale University Press.

Sennett, R. 2008. *The craftsman*. Yale University Press.

Shapin, S. 2017. The superhuman upgrade. A review of Homo Deus: A brief history. *London Review of Books* 39 (14): 29–31.

Sheffi, Y. 2024. Technology is not enough: Potential job displacement in an AI-driven future. *Journal of Supply Chain Management, Logistics and Procurement* 6 (4): 338–351.

Silver, N. 2012. *The signal and the noise: Why so many predictions fail-but some don't*. Penguin.

Spencer, D.A. 2024. AI, automation and the lightening of work. *AI & Society*: 1–11.

Stable Diffusion Launch Announcement. 2022, August 10. https://stability.ai/news/stable-diffusion-announcement. Accessed 1 Jan.

Stanford Vision Lab. 2021. *IMAGENET*. Stanford University, Princeton University. https://image-net.org/. Access 25 Feb 2025.

Stein, M. 2023. US Copyright Office and AI: Notice of inquiry and the Théâtre D'opéra Spatial case. *The Ipkat*, September 27. https://ipkitten.blogspot.com/2023/09/us-copyright-office-and-ai-notice-of.html. Access 25 Feb 2025.

Terzidis, K., F. Fabrocini, and H. Lee. 2023. Unintentional intentionality: Art and design in the age of artificial intelligence. *AI & Society* 38 (4): 1715–1724.

Thomas, A. 2024. A brief history of transhumanism and its critics. In *The politics and ethics of transhumanism*, 1–31. Bristol University Press.

Tirosh-Samuelson, H. 2017. Technologizing transcendence: A critique of transhumanism. In *Religion and human enhancement: Death, values, and morality*, 267–283. Springer.

Toffler, A. 1984. *Future shock*. Bantam.

Tyson, L. D., and J. Zysman. 2022. Automation, AI & work. *Daedalus* 151 (2): 256–271.

van der Vleuten, L. 2014. *Philosophical perspectives on the Singularity*, 1–29. Department of Philosophy, Tilburg University.

Van Dijck, J. 2014. Datafication, dataism and dataveillance: Big data between scientific paradigm and ideology. *Surveillance and Society* 12 (2): 197–208.

Varoufakis, Y. 2023. *Technofeudalism. What killed capitalism*. Random House.

Venus Theory. 2024. AI copyright claimed my last video [video], December 11. YouTube. https://youtu.be/LrkAORPiaEA?si=R2rL4C_GgDxwlCpf.

Voss, P., and M. Jovanovic. 2023. Why we don't have AGI yet. arXiv preprint. arXiv:2308.03598: 1–8.

Watson, D. 2019. The rhetoric and reality of anthropomorphism in artificial intelligence. *Minds and Machines* 29 (3): 417–440.

Zao-Sanders, M. 2025. How people are really using Gen AI in 2025, April 9. https://hbr.org/2025/04/how-people-are-really-using-gen-ai-in-2025.

Zhou, E., and D. Lee. 2024. Generative artificial intelligence, human creativity, and art. *PNAS Nexus* 3 (3): 1–8.

Zirpoli, C. 2023. *Generative artificial intelligence and copyright law*. United States Congress. https://crsreports.congress.gov. Accessed 25 Feb 2025.

Zuboff, S. 2019. The age of surveillance capitalism: The fight for a human future at the new frontier of power. In *Barack Obama's books of 2019*. Profile Books.

Zylinska, J. 2020. *AI art: Machine visions and warped dreams*. Open Humanities Press.

Index[1]

[1] Note: Page numbers followed by 'n' refer to notes.

D. Vargas-Gomez, *The AI Revolution*,
https://doi.org/10.1007/978-3-032-01172-5

The manufacturer's authorised representative in the EU is Springer Nature Customer Service Centre GmbH, Europaplatz 3, 69115 Heidelberg, Germany. If you have any concerns regarding our products, please contact ProductSafety@springernature.com

Printed and bound by CPI Group (UK) Ltd, Croydon, CR0 4YY

05/06/2026

02128857-0002